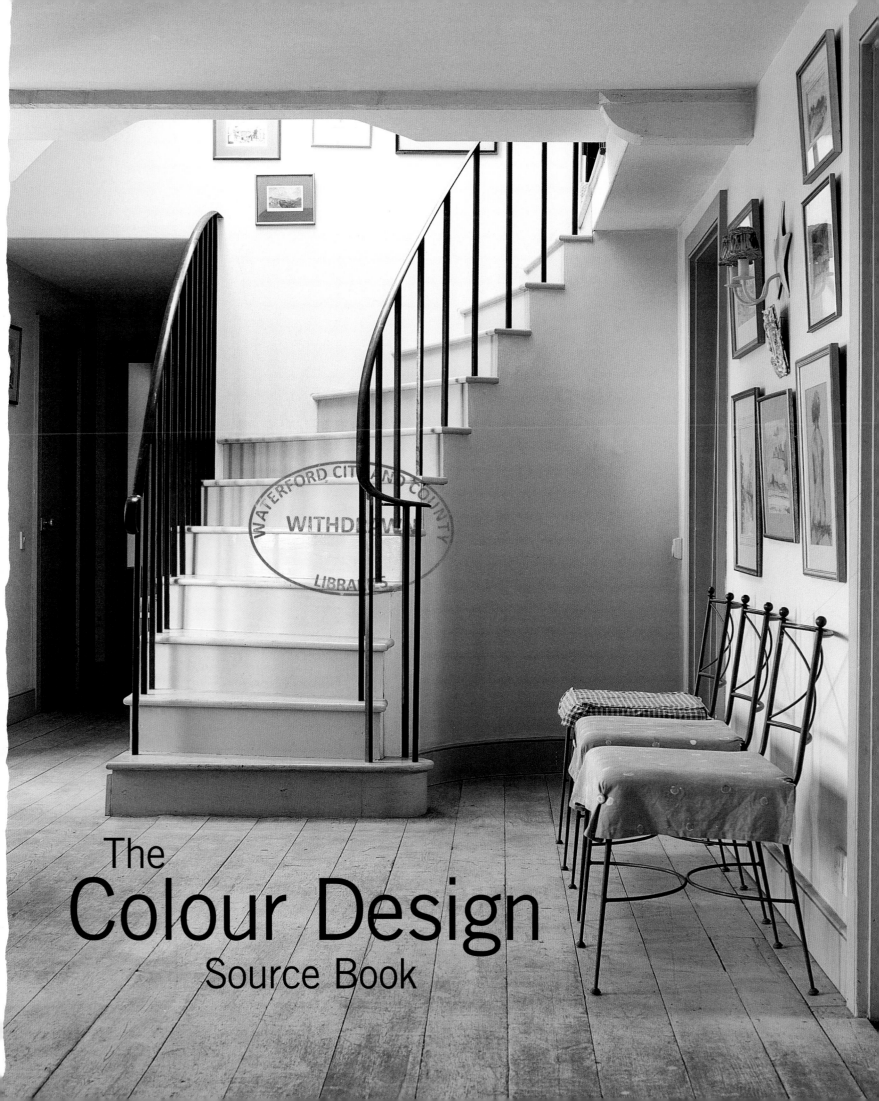

The
Colour Design
Source Book

The Colour Design Source Book

USING FABRICS, PAINTS & ACCESSORIES FOR SUCCESSFUL DECORATING

CAROLINE CLIFTON-MOGG

WITH PHOTOGRAPHY BY ALAN WILLIAMS

RYLAND
PETERS
& SMALL

LONDON NEW YORK

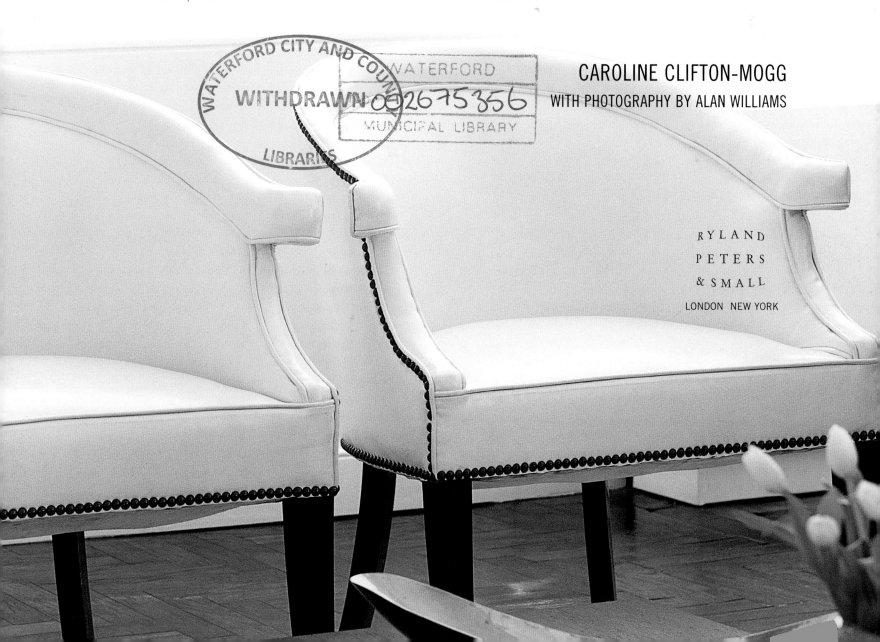

Designer **Catherine Randy**
Senior editor **Sophie Bevan**
Location research manager **Kate Brunt**
Location research assistant **Sarah Hepworth**
Production **Patricia Harrington**
Art director **Gabriella Le Grazie**
Publishing director **Alison Starling**

Additional styling **Marlena Burgess, Emily Jewsbury**
Proofreader **Nikky Twyman**
Indexer **Diana Le Core**

First published in the United Kingdom in 2001
by Ryland Peters & Small
Kirkman House
12–14 Whitfield Street
London W1T 2RP
www.rylandpeters.com
10 9 8 7 6 5 4 3 2 1

ISBN 1 84172 199 9

A CIP record for this book is available from
the British Library.

Printed and bound in China

JACKET PICTURE CREDITS
FRONT: Juan Corbella's apartment
in London designed by HM2,
Richard Webb with Andrew Hanson/
photographer Christopher Drake.
Other photography by Alan Williams.
SPINE: Richard Oyarzarbal's
apartment in London designed by
Urban Research Laboratory
BACK (clockwise from top left):
New York apartment designed by
Bruce Bierman, Lindsay Taylor's
apartment in Glasgow, Katie
Bassford King's house in London
designed by Touch Interior Design,
Donata Sartorio's apartment in
Milan, private apartment in London
designed by Hugh Broughton
Architects, Jennifer & Geoffrey
Symonds' apartment in New York
designed by Jennifer Post Design.

Contents

Introduction

COLOUR IS NOT A LUXURY, IT IS AN ESSENTIAL. IT IS SO MUCH PART OF US AND SO MUCH PART OF OUR LIVES THAT IT IS EASY TO GET OUT OF THE HABIT OF REALLY THINKING ABOUT IT IN A CONCENTRATED MANNER – ABOUT THE EXTRAORDINARY VARIETY OF SHADES AND TONES THAT ARE AVAILABLE, AND WHAT THEY MEAN TO US.

Colour is both the easiest and the hardest element in interior decoration. We accept it totally; we would be lost without it; we expect to use it in our homes, and we expect to use it to best effect. And colour bestows life to everything around it – reason enough to use it and to use it boldly. But too often we take colour for granted, without thinking about how to employ it, or which colours would be right for us to live and work with. Like any other discipline, the use of colour benefits from consideration. Which colours do you empathize with? Which colours do you recall with pleasure or nostalgia – would they work again now? What colours do you wear – your choice of clothes colour, even if you are a dyed-in-the-wool black-only addict, can say a lot about the range of colour – or no colour – you would be happiest living with.

A good way to start the process of choice is to put together a scrapbook of both single colours and colour combinations that you are drawn to – a fragment of material, plain or patterned, old or new; cuttings from magazines showing rooms that use colour in an interesting way; postcards of paintings or illustrations.

That is the first part of choosing the right scheme: to identify the colours that you would be happiest living with. The second part is the practical element: to find out how your choice of colour will look in situ. Try out samples where they will be applied – on the kitchen wall next to the cooker, between the bath and the basin, in the darkest part of the hall. It is vital that a colour is looked at over as long a period, as large an area, and in as many different lights, as possible. It is old advice, but none the less true for that.

BELOW LEFT Some colours work better with wood than others. A brown-red, rich terracotta brings out the colour and grain of the oak door and panelling, as well as of the floor and the furniture, in a way that others colours would not. There is a harmony here between colour and texture.
BELOW Also effective against the dark wooden door and stairs beyond is a kitchen painted in paler colours of the same spectrum: cream cupboards below the wooden worktop are highlighted with upper cupboards in both stone and mushroom. Other doors are brushed aluminium and opaque glass.

OPPOSITE A room of natural neutrals has stone-painted walls hung with muted pastels and watercolours. The wooden eaves are painted white and the carpet is of mushroom wool. This quiet haven is enlivened by a chair covered in what at first appears to be striped material, but which is, of course, a selection of traditional linen glass and tea towels in assorted checks and stripes, some which have even been monogrammed.
ABOVE A muted palette can contain colours other than neutrals, so long as they are of the same tonal values. Here, soft blues, pale lilacs, browns and creams are harmonious together.

The way in which colours relate to each other has long been refined and consigned to charts of mathematical correctness. Although it is doubtful that you would wish to choose colours from a chart, colour relationships are interesting in themselves.

As I say elsewhere, colours are affected not only by the light outside but also by the immediate external surroundings; buildings, trees and grass all alter to a certain degree how the colour inside is perceived.

The earliest facts we are taught about colour – probably at school – are of the importance of primary colours (red, yellow and blue) and how different combinations of two primaries can be mixed to make three secondary colours (purple, orange and green); also that two secondary colours can be mixed to make some of those subtle tertiary colours. Tertiaries can, in fact, be almost indefinite in number, as they can be made from compounds of primaries, secondaries and other tertiaries, in different degrees and combinations. Tertiaries are probably the easiest colours to live with, being subtle combinations which incorporate the strengths of their more strident cousins.

The basic colour wheel is often shown as a brightly coloured segmented circle, and many of us glance at it once, see nothing that particularly appeals, and move on. But the lessons of the colour wheel are very useful when it comes to choosing colours for decorating, particularly when thinking about which colours will work well together. Consider, for example, complementary colours: colours, of equal intensity, that lie opposite each other on the wheel. Amongst the primaries, for example, the opposite to blue on the wheel is orange; the opposite to red is green; and the opposite to yellow is purple. A primary's opposite is the colour which does not have that particular primary in its composition. Decoratively speaking, it is not, of course, necessary to use pillar-box red and emerald green (unless you want to); you could equally use a pinky red and a dark ivy-leaf green. Equally, secondary complementaries are more subtle versions of the primary hues; turquoise, for example, is complementary to tangerine.

Applied to interior decoration, a complementary colour is one that, when used in small doses, draws attention to and grounds the central colour; when mixing colour, a dash of the complementary colour will tone down the stronger colour. Within secondary and tertiary colours, the range of combinations and schemes is infinite, and looking at the different areas of colour – seeing the ones that blend and the ones that contrast – will always light the imagination.

Strictly speaking, white added to an existing colour makes what is called a tint; black added to the same colour makes what is known as a shade and, when both black and white are added, the finished result is called a tone. In reality, these three terms are often misused, and the assumption should not be made that a colour so named will necessarily have been mixed in the way described. Too much white or too much black added to a colour tends to make it misty or murky, with considerable loss of definition.

Tone of colour is also important. Colours which share the same intensity have the same tonal value and tend to work well together. This is a safe guide, but one that must be used with discretion, for tonal harmony is upset by texture – the same colour will look different in paint or linen, for example.

So read your colour chart, spin your colour wheel and study the results, whilst remembering that in the end it is what you like and feel attracted to that will be most successful.

Farbenkugel.

Ansicht des weissen Poles.

Ansicht des schwarzen Poles.

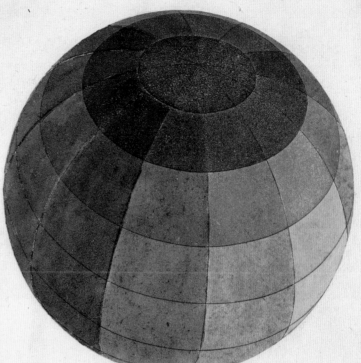

Durchschnitt
durch den Aequator.

Durchschnitt
durch die beyden Pole.

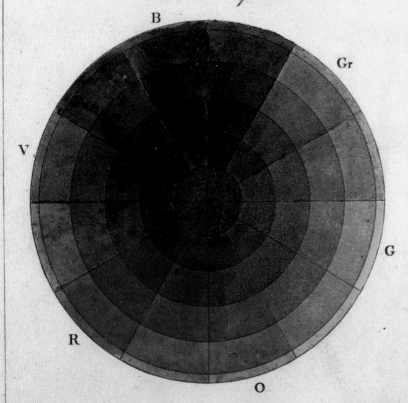

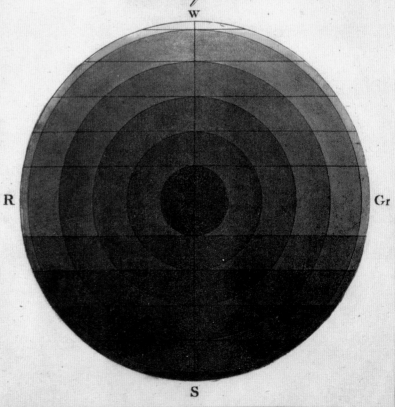

Colour inspirations

A washed-out world of no colour, like an endless low-clouded, grey dawn, is a prospect so depressing and alien that it is difficult to comprehend. We need colour around us, in the natural world and in our homes, on our walls and floors, in our textiles and art.

Yet, despite this need to surround ourselves with colour, finding the right colours for interior decoration can be a daunting prospect, and inspiration can seem far away. But it is not that far. Colour, in all its forms, is interwoven firmly into our lives – throughout history, eye-witness accounts of events, places or people nearly always make some reference to the

colours of the scene described – colour of costume, of decoration and the surrounding landscape. And when colour pigments were difficult to come by, men used what they could find in an inventive and creative way, often turning to nature's combinations as a starting point. As new colours were developed, they were incorporated into daily life – some more readily than others, depending on their scarcity and value. So, when you are searching for ideas, study carefully that which has gone before as well as that which is around you now: decoration, costume, art, nature – inspiration is not as elusive as you might think.

Understanding colour

ACCUSTOMED, AS WE ARE TODAY, TO HAVING LITERALLY HUNDREDS OF PAINT COLOURS AVAILABLE AT THE TOUCH OF THE BUTTON ON AN AUTOMATIC MIXING MACHINE, AS WELL AS THE CHOICE OF THOUSANDS OF TEXTILES, PRINTED AND WOVEN IN BRIGHT DESIGNS, IT IS INSTRUCTIVE TO THINK OF THE LENGTHS – THE SHEER INVENTIVENESS AND RESOURCEFULNESS – TO WHICH PEOPLE HAVE GONE IN ORDER TO BRING COLOUR INTO THEIR LIVES.

All paint colours and dyes as we know them today are derived from mixing pigments with a binding medium, which allows them to be transferred onto a surface. Until the middle of the nineteenth century, when rapid chemical advances were made and pigments began to be produced synthetically, colours were naturally obtained from the minerals and earth, vegetables and plants that were available. Early mediums included egg for the making of tempera, and later oil.

There are about eight earth pigments, including sienna, ochre and umber, and these could be mixed with minerals like iron oxide and copper-based pigments to give a range of colours that suited every need. Roots like indigo were used, too. Rare, precious – and correspondingly expensive – colours were also made: rich ultramarine blue from crushed, ground lapis lazuli, and the brightest green from malachite treated in the same way. The tones and hues of colours differed, of course, from region to region, which is why we associate today certain colours – particularly those made from earth and clay – with certain areas.

Yarn, too, was rarely left in its natural, undyed state. From flowers and fruit to roots and bark – and even shellfish – dyes were squeezed from the natural world to bring colour to the neutral tones of wool, linen and cotton. In fact, textiles, rather than flat planes of colour seen on walls, are often the starting point for colour inspirations. Historically, fashion has inspired choices of decorative colours, and it still does. To go to a museum of costume or an archive exhibition can be positively regenerating –

the colour of embroidered threads on a eighteenth-century brocade waistcoat, the woven designs on a nineteenth-century 'kirking' shawl. Modern fashion can be equally thought-provoking – both street and couture fashion are constantly looking for new ways to use colour, many of which can be translated into decorative terms. This is also true of accessories: many couture houses, for example, once designed silk headscarves (an essential for the elegant woman). Painted designs were hand-screened onto silk squares, and the thought and subtlety of colour that went into these period pieces are text book examples of the use of colour in our time.

BELOW The artists of the Impressionist movement used colour to convey the spirit of the immediacy of the natural world. The landscape in Pierre Auguste Renoir's *Chemin montant dans les hautes herbes* (c. 1876) is painted in greens, yellows, blacks and whites – with dashes of red, the complementary colour to green, introduced at strategic points.

Paintings are another fertile source of colour inspiration. This applies not only to the colours that artists have used harmoniously, but also in the way in which groups, such as the Impressionists and the Post-Impressionists, used paint in a very precise manner, putting small dashes of colours separately, but next to each other, so that in close-up a dense mosaic of identifiable colour can be seen, whilst at a distance something completely different appears.

Familiarity breeds, if not contempt, then at least laziness. We often accept what we see around us without analysing why we are pleased by one thing and dismayed by another. All artists – lesser and greater – look, and really try to see what it is they are looking at. And, to find inspiration from a painting, look at it again, and again, to see not only *how* the colours work together but also *why* they work.

Whether you find your inspiration in a museum or an art gallery, from the pages of a magazine or walking down the street, the interesting thing is that each and every source, indeed all applied colour, is based on

LEFT In the Renaissance painter, Andrea Mantegna's (1431–1506) magnificent portrait of Cardinal Carlo de Medici, the eye is drawn to the richness of colour in the robes, emphasized by the thin circle of gold at the neck.
BELOW *The Card Players* by Paul Cézanne (1839–1906) is a wonderfully rich, dark study. Browns, greens, oranges, yellows and reds all work together with touches of black, white and – surprisingly – pink.

what we see around us in the natural world. When we are inspired by the tones in a painting, we can remember that the artist arrived at that particular effect through his wish to recreate the shades and tones of the world around him. These are the subtleties and nuances that every artist, from the first cave painter onwards, has struggled to interpret and develop. From Piero della Francesca, Fra Angelico and Giotto to Titian, Gainsborough and Reynolds, Renoir and Cézanne to Van Gogh and Matisse – all of them spent their working lives analysing and refining the best way to use their brush strokes and the colour they had – or could make – to show the tones and colours of nature at their truest.

It would be hard to find a better set of instructors, so we too perhaps should take the colour combinations of nature as our first point of inspirational departure. The most important thing is to look – *really* look – at the natural colours around us. Everything – a leaf, a flower, a stone – is affected by the colour of the day, the strength of the sunlight at the moment we are

THIS PAGE A bed of herbs in greens from mauve to grey to white; tree bark in every gold-toned variation; startling narcissus flowers against blue-green leaves; and the fragile beauty of a poppy, its centre of delicately striped red and yellow, encircled in green, and surrounded by soft white petals tipped with smoke grey – nature never stops teaching us about colour.

looking at it. Light affects everything: The sky itself is a perfect example: look at the sky on a sunlit day to see how many changes in tone there are, from the deepness of bowl over our heads down to the muted tones of the horizon, and the way that a passing cloud will change and intensify those colours.

As far as colour combinations go, whether subtle or striking, nature, even in miniature, never gets it wrong: recollect the face of a viola with its intense shades of pure purple, mauve, yellow and white; an olive or willow leaf – cool, grey-silver on one side, a harmonizing grey-green on the other; old-fashioned pinks with a clear pink petal that contrasts with a dark blood-red centre, framed by a grey-blue leaf; a white hydrangea as it slowly ages into a watered lime green, touched with dashes of mauve-pink and claret. And, on a more awesome scale, the colour of a New England autumn – a travel cliché perhaps, but only because the flamboyantly bright reds, russets, ochres, oranges and toffee browns still make the eye stop with surprise and delight. Or, on a quieter level, there is a traditional English rural, wooded landscape, where nothing but green is seen, but with so many subtle variations on a theme that it seems as if an entire paint box has been employed. The variety of colour, of contrast and of tone to be found in nature can never fail to astonish and delight.

In the same way that light changes everything, we see both outside and inside, so lands of light inspire us with the colour that we experience there. In many parts of the world, decorative colours are natural pigments used in their full intensity, rather than the diluted colours so often seen in northern Europe and North America. In India, for example – where the trees, shrubs and flowers are vivid and striking, and the palaces of Rajasthan have vibrant interiors with walls studded with bright jewels set against marble – dyes and paints bring colour to everyday surfaces. These invigorating, exciting pigments have a sharpness and a brightness that more than hold their own under the harsh sunlight, although they might be difficult to live with in more shadowed climes.

In the Caribbean, the fierceness of the light highlights paintwork that was originally painted in cheerful bright pinks, mauves and blues, but which speedily fades to softer shades that harmonize with a natural background of blue water, yellow-green palms and impossibly pale gold sand. Caribbean inspiration could also be found in the show-off sunsets of orange, fire red, shell pink, cream, pale yellow and a touch of old silver, all set against a blackening sea.

The colours of southern France, in the hills of Provence and by the Mediterranean, are another colour inspiration. The sun shines brightly here, but the light

is diffused and softer than that of the Caribbean. This softness is reflected in the tones of the indigenous trees and plants. There is a subtlety in the colours of the olive trees, the fields of lavender and the shutters of faded blue, mauve or green against an ochre or sienna background. These colours translate with comparative ease to more temperate atmospheres.

Lavender fields, in fact, are good examples of the effect natural light has on our surroundings. Compare the lavender fields of Provence and those of England. Both grow the same crop, but the first impression of the colour of the fields is very different. In the softer, diffused light of England, the lavender looks equally soft, equally diffused; under the clear bright light of southern France, however, the same lavender reaches intensely towards you, emphasizing its brightness and clarity and sheer shock value.

Not only do these international examples provide inspiration for colour combinations, but they also high-light the need to consider the natural light in a space before selecting colours. All the colours in your scheme will be affected by what one might call external influences: what is outside the window, whether it is the strength of the sunlight, the colour of the sky, the surrounding buildings, or nature, green and in the raw.

ABOVE Certain colours and tones are indelibly associated with places and countries. The faded earth red of this house on a Venetian canal sums up much of Italy; indeed its commercial counterpart is sometimes known as Tuscan red. It is the naturalness of this colour which attracts, the way it seems to be part of the very fabric of the house, brighter, newer patches next to older, faded pink areas. The traditional dark green used for the shutters enhances the colour.
RIGHT Very much a colour of the sands and the desert, the warm ochre of this Moroccan mausoleum again seems to exude from the walls, rather than being imposed onto them. The colours of the two different tile designs blend and tone with the wall colour in perfect harmony.

LEFT The embellishment of one's surroundings is one of man's most primitive inclinations. To this end, colour has always excited, and artists and craftsmen have used it in profusion. Men, beasts and religious subjects cover every surface of this Norwegian room, decorated in the eighteenth century in a style known as 'rosemaling'.
BELOW The Ancient Romans used profuse and strong colour inside their houses. This room in the Villa of Mysteries in Pompeii shows the women's rite of the sacred Agape boldly painted, employing deep red and black extensively, the wall divided into broad panels.

Colour through history

COLOUR HAS BEEN A KEY ELEMENT IN INTERIOR DESIGN EVER SINCE MAN FIRST DISCOVERED HOW TO USE PIGMENTS DERIVED FROM THE EARTH AND VEGETABLE MATTER. THE WAYS MAN HAS SINCE USED THIS TECHNOLOGY TO ADORN HIS SURROUNDINGS IS A LESSON TO US ALL IN THE POWER AND IMPORTANCE OF COLOUR IN OUR HOMES.

No sooner had early man come in from the cold than he began to draw markings on his cave walls, pounding and mashing the earth and vegetable matter to produce the colours he desired. Even the earliest cave paintings – like those executed at Lascaux in France – show traces of colour within them.

The Ancient Egyptians were possibly the first to appreciate the power of colour fully, and, from the ornate sarcophagi to the richly frescoed interiors, colour was an integral part of Egyptian art. They used mainly primary colours: red was made from haematite, an iron ore; yellow, from the mineral orpiment; and blue was made either from the mineral cobalt or from copper. Green was also used, made from the semi-precious mineral, malachite; and white was used to vary the tones of these colours. The Egyptians also often outlined their fresco paintings in a vegetable or bone black.

It is hard to know exactly how extensively the Greeks used colour in decoration, as very few domestic buildings survive and there are no known pictorial records. We do, however, know that Greek houses were relatively simple inside – much of daily life was pursued in the open – and that they used the paint they had boldly in one or more colours, most often red, which may be combined with white, yellow and black.

The Romans loved colour and used it with confidence in their homes. Rooms were painted by applying single colours to different areas. The walls of a reception room might be divided into three sections – dado, middle and entablature. Dados were usually dark, even black, with simple geometric designs; the central section was often painted purple, green, blue or yellow and might have descriptive scenes or landscapes on it, surrounded with panels filled with decorative motifs; and above might be a painted frieze of some description, often on a white background. The murals were bright and literally shone, a finish perhaps achieved by polishing the painted surface. And, in Pompeii, where the interiors were even more sophisticated, colour was used lavishly, often mixed to produce softer tones that worked together in a harmonious way.

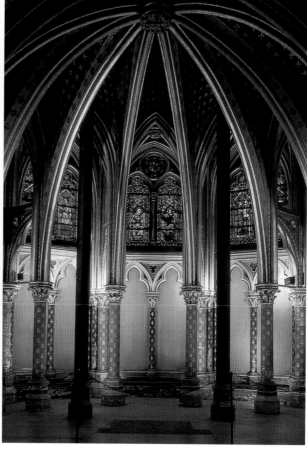

Colour was everywhere in medieval Europe: Romanesque and Gothic interiors throbbed with colour, profuse and brilliant. It is almost a cliché to say that the grey interiors we see today were once of bursting brightness: colour was applied to stone and wood as well as walls and ceilings; when the stone was decorated, the attendant bosses, pendants and carvings were also painted. Even the undersides of arches and beams were painted and gilded, as were the spaces between. At first, colour – often white or blue – was applied en masse, then picked out with bright tints and enriched with gold flowers, stars and other motifs. Over time, the schemes became more sophisticated and clever. Curious – and surprisingly daring – colour combinations began to appear. They used black, white and red; red, bright blue and gold. Narrow bands of colour wound round timbers like early barber-shop poles, and stars were painted in gold onto heavenly blue ceilings. They used counter-changing:

one panel might be painted white with black decoration; another, black with white designs. And artists employed trompe l'oeil, as curled scrolls with writing on were seemingly attached to beams and rafters. Exuberant and free-flowing as it all looked, there were distinct and clever rules that were employed to ensure harmony. The rich colours used, which included red, blue, green and purple, were invariably separated from each other with thin lines of gold, yellow, black or white. Very bright colours were often painted on backgrounds of yellow or gold, white or silver or black, which not only gave them prominence, but also contained them, not allowing the feast of pattern and colour to confuse the eye.

To see one of these interiors restored – Sainte Chapelle in Paris, for example – is breathtaking. The richness, the imagination, the ideas, are startling. Not only are the best of these medieval interiors historically fascinating, they are also fuel for your own decorative

ABOVE *The Baptism of Christ* by Piero della Francesca, painted in the fifteenth century, demonstrates brilliantly the care which early artists took to make and use the right colours. Although the colours we see today have changed over the centuries, the choice, contrast and tonal harmony of the colour is as pleasing today as it must have been when first painted.

LEFT In this Elizabethan dining hall in Brookgate, on the border between England and Wales, the panels of plaster between the wooden beams have been coloured with a traditional sienna pigment. Domestic sixteenth-century interiors were usually far more highly coloured and decorated than they now appear to us.

inspiration, for, although such design may seem far removed from decorative schemes of today, inspiration lies in the combination of colour, the use of pattern and the discipline behind the free-flowing designs.

Religious symbolism played its part, too, in the chosen colours of early, and indeed later, artists. White stands for light and purity; blue represents contemplative faith, the heavens, and is of course the colour of the Virgin Mary; red stands for militant faith, genius, fire and charity; green is for hope and rebirth; and black is for mourning.

From medieval times onwards, chemists and artists were mixing pigments together, as well as experimenting with different minerals and chemicals to try to increase the range of colour available. And, by the fifteenth century, there were many more colours in pigment form than ever before. Most widely used still were the earth colours: raw and burnt sienna, raw and burnt umber, and the ochres. These were cheap and easily obtainable from the earth, but now they were mixed with other compounds to produce a far greater variety of shades and hues.

Even then, fashion affected the popularity of various colours. In England, for example, the livery colours of the Tudors were green, white and red, and these shades became extremely fashionable throughout the reigns of the Tudor kings and queens. At that time, colour was used both inside and out: Tudor gardens had brightly painted wooden rails and tall wooden posts topped with painted and carved heraldic figures. With painted and gilded wood and plaster inside, as well as walls of embroidered and woven hangings, how cheerful and colourful life must have looked.

The Renaissance, particularly as it developed in Italy, influenced many areas of artistic life, including the use and choice of colour throughout Europe. Artists like Raphael (1483–1520) and his contemporaries rediscovered in the ruins of Ancient Rome vestiges of classical decoration – the grotesques (so called because these designs were originally discovered in grottoes of excavated villas), the murals, the wonderful decorative flights of fancy. Inspired by what they saw, they painted similar decoration

LEFT The decoration of Ham House, outside London, home of the Duke and Duchess of Lauderdale at the end of the seventeenth century, was known even in its own time as being the last word in taste and fine decorative techniques.

TOP The hall of the Joseph Webb house in Wethersfield, Connecticut, built in the late eighteenth century, is painted with oil paints in the original colours of Georgian green and pale lilac. Green, made from an expensive pigment, was particularly popular amongst the wealthy.

ABOVE Although certain pigments were expensive, others were cheaper and widely used, particularly in less-important, secondary rooms. In this colonial house in New York State, the woodwork has been painted in inexpensive Spanish brown.

in new buildings, such as the Villa Madama and the Loggie of the Vatican. In fact, Renaissance artists covered most interiors with bright decoration: walls and richly carved, embellished wooden ceilings, colour and gilding were everywhere. Many more pigments were used during the Renaissance, and black and white were added to other colours in measured quantities to increase the range of tones. Such colour and designs continued to influence the decorative arts for hundreds of years.

In northern Europe, where the light was not so strong, and the temperament quieter, less vivid colours were preferred. In England, Renaissance influence permeated slowly through domestic decoration, and surfaces became increasingly ornamented with frescoed and painted walls and ceilings, highlighted by judicious gilding. The seventeenth century was a time of monumental interior architecture, with pilasters and coffering, and wall paintings executed on canvas.

The new settlers in America, however, had not the same luxury of choice where colour was concerned. There, pigments and dyes for paints and textiles were prised from the land and boiled and beaten into submission for use at home. For the early settlers, nothing was to be wasted, and cloth brought from Europe was recycled into useful household goods, whilst linen and wool and cotton were woven and dyed, using all parts of the plant from the root to the leaf, the nuts and the bark.

By the eighteenth century, there were two standards of colour. For most people, cheap pigments and mediums were used; houses were limewashed outside, and coated with distemper inside. Distemper was ground chalk mixed with glue size and tinted with a pigment. Usually the pigment was an earth colour, but sometimes something a little more exotic was used – ox blood, for example, gave a fetching rusty pink. It was a different story for the wealthy. Throughout the eighteenth century, the range of colours available became increasingly sophisticated. In the early 1700s, many interiors had painted wood panelling; any visible plaster was painted with oil-based paint in neutrals, like white or stone, with the

panelling in wood tones, like buff, walnut brown and chocolate. However, as the century progressed and plaster replaced panelling, paint was increasingly popular – for the rich. Those wonderful colours appeared that we now associate with the eighteenth century in general, and with the designs of Robert Adam in particular – colours like pea green, sky blue, light pink and lemon, all achieved by mixing different pigments and experimenting with proportions. Deeper tones of green and blue were still the most expensive, and therefore the most desired.

During the seventeenth (and certainly by the eighteenth) century, supremacy in the decorative arts had shifted from Italy to France, and the French remained at the forefront of interior decoration and style until the late 1800s. Over the period marked by the reigns of the four Louis, there were various popular colour schemes: Louis XIII (1601–43) introduced paintings as decoration, with both floral designs and figurative pictures; whilst under Louis XIV (1638–1715) colour became lighter and brighter, and houses decorated during the reign of Louis XV (1710–74) often combined gold and pale colours in sinuous rococo designs. The truncated reign of Louis XVI (1754–93) saw the first steps towards

a new classical simplicity. Many of the colours used during the period – white, pale pink, blue, slate grey and soft browns, often with touches of gold – are still thought of today as quintessentially French.

By the end of the eighteenth (and the beginning of the nineteenth) century, the decorative style in England, France and Italy had come to embrace the lure of the antique, and both Regency and Empire interiors were often decorated with strong colours, like black and terracotta red – many of them imitating the deep pigments that had been used by the Ancient Greeks and Romans. The classical references were also repeated in the way the walls were coloured, with the skirting, dado wall and cornice all decorated to recall the form of the classical column. Many of these colours were bright, but they were still relatively soft, coming as they did from natural pigments.

All that was to change: the advances of the industrial revolution were about to play their part in the history of colour. Paint technology was advancing, synthetic pigments were under experimentation and, in the mid-1800s, new colours exploded into the world, some shown for the first time in their startling glory at the Great Exhibition of 1851 in London. Now

ABOVE LEFT The delicacy of decoration in eighteenth-century France was appreciated throughout Europe. Here, a salon in a small eighteenth-century chateau is decorated entirely with carved and gilded panelling on a soft grey background.
ABOVE During the mid-eighteenth century, Robert Adam, after spending much time in Italy, introduced into England the delicate, colourful interior schemes that we associate with him today, such as this for Northumberland House in London. His schemes often included designs for furniture and carpets as well.

BELOW In general, as the twentieth century progressed, the use of colour in design became simpler than it had been in preceding centuries. Artists like David Hockney, whose *Beverley Hills Housewife* (painted in 1966) is seen here, used flat planes of colour in a way that influenced other artists and designers of the time.

there were purples, lilacs, salmon pinks, oranges, acid yellows, and many greens, both bright and dark. They were used with abandon on walls and ceilings, and the surrounding woodwork, too, was often painted in a dark heavy colour. This was the period when, for the first time ever, mass production meant that many of the elements of a decorated interior, which had previously been available only to the wealthy, could now be bought by all. Not only the new paints, but also textiles, floor coverings and wallpaper – most of them brightly patterned – could be bought at reasonable prices. Unfortunately, the replacement of the craftsman by the machine meant that the quality was often suspect, and the schemes loud and garish.

The nineteenth century was not entirely a place of the bright, brash and bold. With other like-minded souls, the architect and ornamental designer, Owen Jones (1809–74), sought to redefine the principles of design, pattern and colour. In 1856, his influential book *Grammar of Ornament* was first published, which presented thousands of ornamental motifs drawn from the ancient world through to the Renaissance. A few years later, the British artist and craftsman, William Morris (1834–96), developed these ideas further, forming his own, now famous, movement and manufacturing company, introducing (or rather re-introducing) the idea of simplicity in design and the use of natural dyes and pigments.

These softer, clearer colours survived the transition from the nineteenth to the twentieth century and were echoed by some modern designers. As the century advanced, the new profession of 'interior designers' espoused simplified design and decorative schemes and new attitudes to colour, which ranged from the studies in neutrals promoted by fashionable decorators of the 1920s and 1930s to the bright, almost naïve colour preferred by the Omega movement and used with abandon on every flat surface.

The twentieth century became a time for everything to be tried – from the 1960s, where fashion, decoration, textiles (even furnishing accessories) were suffused with bright bold, often harsh colour, to periods where the virtues of natural colour and textures were much vaunted. Which brings us to our own, young century: today we seem to have a new attitude towards colour – an attitude of no attitude. We seem easy with it, and its availability has meant that we swing effortlessly through colour phases and fashions – sometimes bright and strong, sometimes pale and reflective. The big difference seems to be not so much in the colours used, but in the quality and texture of those colours. And there is more to come ....

Colours explored

An infinite variety of tones and shades can be created from combining primary colours and from adding white and black, which of course makes choosing the colour you like not quite as simple as it first sounds.

When deciding what colour to use in the home, first think about what colours – or tones of colour – instinctively appeal to you when you see them by chance. The sort of colours that you like to wear can be helpful here, although that is not to say that if you are wedded to black then your home should be nothing but an underworld symphony.

Prismatic colours are violet, indigo, blue, green, yellow, orange and red – the seven colours seen from the decomposition of a ray of light when passed through the prism. The colours of the spectrum have varying tones because our eyes are more sensitive to some colours than to others. Yellow is always light in tone because our eyes are most sensitive to it, whilst pure red and pure blue appear the darkest. In dim light, our eyes are most sensitive to green and blue, and any red becomes very dark.

Nuances of colour – all the subtle hues and tones we see around us – are made by adding basic yellows, reds, blues and blacks, either to each other or to white; and, depending on the balance of pigments combined, either cold or warm tones of colour are created.

Originally, artists used basic earth and metal pigments and experimented mixing different pigments together, as well as mixing them with white, to arrive at the colour they wanted. Today, the large paint companies do the same thing commercially, and on a huge scale, using modern, synthetic pigments; but I think it helps to remember that every colour is simply a combination of other colours and that, depending on the strength and colour values of the originals, different new colours can be created in profusion.

OPPOSITE Natural tones are as beautiful as bright colours. Soft and welcoming, they work particularly well when they take their cue from the colour of natural materials, such as the golden stone of this country fireplace.
PREVIOUS PAGE The tones used in this bathroom are carefully chosen to work together. The walls are deep red, but with a brown-terracotta tinge, which is complemented perfectly by the natural wood of the wash basin surround and wooden frame of the mirror. The beaten metal basin adds a sharp tone of contrast.

Whites, greys and blacks

Whites, greys, blacks – this is where the story of neutrals begins. The colours we broadly think of as neutrals – all those soft subtle shades without which decorating the home would be impossible – are colours that are usually made by adding white to basic pigments. These neutral shades should not be dismissed out of hand. Neither dull nor boring, they are in fact the most sophisticated colours around. Many of us start our lives in colour using shades that get quickly to the point – the sort of colours that need no introduction. But, as we learn more about colour, we begin to appreciate the subtlety of so-called neutrals – their air of quiet calm and confidence. They are not primaries, nor secondaries, nor even complementary – they are nuances of colour.

Pure whites and off-whites

YOU MIGHT THINK THAT WHITE IS WHITE IS WHITE, BUT THERE IS MUCH MORE TO THE STORY. IT SEEMS SO EASY TO SAY WHAT WHITE IS, BUT ACTUALLY IT'S EASIER TO SAY WHAT IT ISN'T. IT ISN'T A FLAT SHEET OF NOTHING; IT IS A COLOUR THAT PRODUCES EMOTIONS AND FEELINGS, AND WARM WHITES ARE VERY DIFFERENT FROM COOL WHITES.

ABOVE As glossy as a dark, frozen pond, the highly varnished almost-black wood of the floor is in striking and telling contrast to the ice-white sheen of the walls and woodwork. A white-covered day-bed sits beneath the window, and grounding the design is a small cabinet, which brings curves into an otherwise linear scheme.

Pure white on its own, unrelieved and bouncing back off the walls around you, only ever works in countries where strong sunlight and, even more important, deep shadows are apparent every day. Likewise, snowy marble is only acceptable to our eyes when it has become a little spoiled by time. It is important to recognize that pure white is *not* brilliant white; nothing except a packet of optically bleached detergent and

builders' all-purpose paint are brilliant white, and this artificial shade has no place in interior decoration.

Most artists and decorators will always use more than one shade of white. The late interior designer John Fowler, for example, sometimes employed ten shades of white – pure white, broken whites, off-whites – that he might put together in one room – and that would be only for the paintwork. Fowler used these tones of pure white and off-white on the wood-work, using the skirting, dado rail and panelled doors as his canvases. There he highlighted, shaded and added depth and variation in almost imperceptible fashion to create a subtle and interesting end result.

If you want to use and combine off-whites in the same manner, vary the finish as well as the tone – paint some surfaces in a matt finish, some in a soft sheen, with perhaps one that shines reflectively. Experiment with balancing the tones and emphasizing one feature whilst minimizing another. Bear in mind, too, that whites, like most other colours, take on a hint of other colours they are paired with, depending on how they are used, what surface they cover and what the prevailing natural or artificial light is.

LEFT If you are using a colour entirely on its own – particularly such a stark, uncompromising colour as white – it is important to emphasize the purity of that colour by introducing something strong in contrast. Here, the fact that these chairs are not only white, but white leather to boot, demands a striking addition, which is supplied by the plentiful use of traditional brass upholstery studs that closely follow the lines of the chair.

WARM WHITES

Warm whites smack of luxury – ivory, buttermilk, pale cream – and I would like to have them all round me constantly; all, that is, except magnolia, for which (along with brilliant white) I have a complete loathing,

THIS PAGE Throughout the room, nothing detracts from the disciplined and creative use of white, which is, however, emphasized by the judicious use of black. All white schemes – particularly one as uncompromising as this one – need grounding. Against white walls and white window blinds and on a glossy dark floor, the white sofa and white leather chairs contrast with a dark-wood and chrome Italian coffee table and a glossy ebony bar, as well as the dark studding on the shiny leather chairs. The effect is soothing rather than stark.

Different textures make this scheme interesting: a contemporary Italian sofa by B&B Italia, upholstered in white, is combined with severe white leather chairs on a warm white flat-weave wide rug, which is flecked with dashes of neutral colour. A mirror in the background reflects even more white light.

White is pristine; white is fresh — there is no cleaner, fresher colour. But, if nothing but white is to be used, keep it soft and add some tones that reflect a little warmth.

ABOVE LEFT As almost nothing in interior decoration looks worse than grubby white upholstery, a pure-white decorative scheme is not for everyone; indeed it is only for the very tidy few. However, in this light, bright Manhattan apartment, a successful exercise in using white has been conducted, which cannot fail to appeal.

RIGHT In the same way that white flowers of different shades and tones will all work together in a garden devoted to them alone, so do different whites work successfully in all-white interiors. The varying tones to be found in white flowers — yellow, green, blue, pink, grey — add a subtle note to man-made schemes.

probably because they are both associated with that most depressing of phrases: 'a builder's finish'.

Warm whites are soft and calming. These are the whites that are mixed with a touch of raw sienna or with raw umber; yellow ochre mixed with white adds warm tones to make pale creams and vellums – these, in their deeper and still-warmer shades appear again in the chapter on creams and browns (see pages 40–51). The decorator's term is 'broken white' and, if you are using ready-mixed paint, then those who know, swear by a white that has just a touch of yellow added to it to give the perfect warm hue.

White will always work in a scheme with one other colour – any other colour. Soft whites, particularly when two or three are gathered together, make other colours sing. The white will reflect tones of the second colour within itself, so choose your white with this in mind. If the other shade is orange-red, for example, then a warm white with a dash of yellow will work, rather than a grey-toned white. Needless to say, warm whites work better than cool tones in a cold climate or in rooms that don't get a great deal of sunlight.

COOL WHITES

If warm whites are soft, then cool whites are sophisticated – sometimes very sophisticated. Cool whites are not pure, nor are they brilliant whites; they are off-whites produced by combining pure white pigment with a dash of one of the blacks or blues or perhaps a touch of cold yellow. These combinations

THIS PAGE When fitted kitchens were first designed, the newest and best were nearly always all-white, presumably to strengthen the contrast between the inefficient past and the streamlined future. Today, they can still shock with their single-minded modernity. This white example – in the same apartment as the living room of the previous pages – is pristine and glossy. Shiny white walls compete with reflective surfaces on the chairs and table as well as the kitchen cabinets. The only contrast comes in the mottled tile floor.

produce subtle tones that range from pearl to putty to parchment.

Using a palette of cool whites together means mixing them in all elements of the room, because, as decorator Syrie Maugham demonstrated in the 1930s, a white-neutral palette only really works in a room where, not only is there a strong contrast of shade and light, but also where each different texture is also strongly emphasized. As she advocated, so designers follow today the idea of rough with smooth, leather with velvet, stone with lacquer. It must be said that mixing cool whites together in a room is probably not the easiest of schemes for decorative beginners. Because of their pale subtlety, their almost evanescent qualities, they do need to be handled with confidence.

Cool whites include that particular soft white touched with green, which looks so right in houses of a certain age (namely dating from the eighteenth and nineteenth centuries); and the grey-white that is indelibly associated with sophisticated French interiors of the eighteenth and nineteenth centuries. These cool whites are so subtle that, on entering a room, it is not always instantly possible to name and describe the colour around you – which is what makes them so useful. Think of the colour of a pearl or a piece of almost-white jade or alabaster. Grey-white, cool blue-white (not to be confused with the unmentionable brilliant white) and real snow-white are also tones that we often associate with Scandinavian decoration.

Most colour schemes, and that includes those which are predominantly white, are improved with a dash of a contrasting shade. But contrast, in this instance, does not have to be translated as strong or bright. A flash of red or green will highlight white, but so too will softer shades – rose pink or watered turquoise-blue.

THIS PAGE In this all-white kitchen, although there is no apparent contrast of strong colour, there is instead a contrast of tone and texture. Like frosted ice in a cave of snow, the appliances – the hob, the microwave oven and so on – are all in stainless steel with a brushed finish, as is the deep splash-back behind the equipment. The units themselves are white, as are the walls. The worktop is in dense white Corian and, in front of the units, is a long dining table made of polished, dark wood, which is surrounded with grey-painted chairs. The effect is far from frosty.

Greys and blacks

AT MANY PERIODS THROUGH DECORATIVE HISTORY, GREY AND BLACK HAVE BEEN TREATED WITH CAUTION. BLACK, IN PARTICULAR, HAS MORE OFTEN BEEN UTILIZED AS AN ACCENT OR AS A DEVICE TO EMPHASIZE THE VALUE AND STRENGTH OF OTHER COLOURS OR ARCHITECTURAL FEATURES, THAN AS A COLOUR IN ITS OWN RIGHT.

In fashion terms, all colours have their moment and now is the moment for grey, in every shade from off-white to nearly black. Grey is often thought of as boring or even bland. For many years it languished, written off as a dark and dismal 'bachelor's colour'. It is true that, in cooler climes, it can be a difficult colour to decorate with, although the French have always appreciated the beauty and practical applications of grey, which they tint with pinks and blues, making it a warm and accommodating shade that both flatters and complements other colours.

WARM GREYS

Warm greys can make an immensely flattering background for furniture and textiles; think of them used in a bedroom, mixed with deep pinks or spiky yellows. And one of the most flattering of colour combinations, both in fashion and in decoration, is warm pale grey with warm but pale shell pink.

Perhaps to some, greys are a little Edwardian, but they are none the worse for that – Edwardian elegance is much admired, and grey can be part of some of the most sophisticated decorative fancies. Think of grisaille work – panelling and trophies, painted as

THIS PAGE This bedroom is an object lesson in how to use greys and blacks together to achieve a welcoming, warm and interesting room. As a background, the walls are painted in a warm white, and the half-tester bed is in black, with grey bed-linen which, in this setting, is warmer than traditional white. Bedside furniture and lamps are dark-toned, and all the accessories are in tones of black and grey, from the wool damask throw to the cushions in smoky fur and black leather. Once again, the combination and contrast of texture is of the essence in achieving an easy balance between style and comfort.

THIS PAGE In this large open-plan living area, grey is teamed with white, grounded by an uncarpeted floor of polished boards made from a rich-toned African hardwood. The effect is uncompromising and is made livable with by the fact that the grey upholstery of the seating unit is, in texture, matt and warm. There is little decoration in the room except for a painting which is predominantly in sharp pinks – one of the colours that looks best with grey. A suspended white wall hangs from the angled ceiling, and behind, on a raised dais, a low fire adds more warmth to this very definite and contemporary scheme.

RIGHT AND BELOW RIGHT Dove grey is one of the most attractive of greys. Soft and accommodating, never strident, it is a perfect background colour for displaying objects or pictures. On this rustic internal verandah in an apartment in Milan, it is the ideal foil for a display of cheerfully patterned porcelain plates.

OPPOSITE In this Paris living room, the walls are painted the lightest of greys as a background colour. They have then been inset with hand-painted panels of stylized birds and branches, which are edged with gold. Everything has been chosen to coordinate with gentle charm. On the mantelpiece is a pair of soft grey-white bisque porcelain figures, and against the panels is an antique chair covered in grey-and-white ticking. Flat grey woodwork – softer than the same shade would be in a gloss finish – and old parquet flooring complete the picture. Note the fillet of gold edging the opening of the fireplace and echoing the gold moulding around the panels.

trompe l'oeil ovals directly onto plaster and wood, and executed entirely in greys. Think of fawn and taupe or noted interior designer Nancy Lancaster's 'elephant's breath' (well, one knows what she meant). Like all neutrals, they are subtle to a fault; think of wood smoke – almost colourless and nearly here, nearly there.

COOL GREYS

An absolute and obvious rule of using colour is that any cool colour should be used with caution in cold rooms and under cold lights, and that rule particularly applies to greys. The closer a cool grey is to black, the more light it absorbs and the more it demands from its surroundings; conversely, the more white it contains, the more accessible – but colder – it appears.

It is strange that many of us have a problem using grey in interiors when we are so wedded to it in our clothes; there is barely a wardrobe around that does not hold some item of clothing in the ever-useful,

Gold, used judiciously and with a light hand, is a wonderful foil for cool grey.

perennially flattering grey. Thinking in fashion and textile terms is one way to visualize the range of grey: flannel, angora, satin. The natural world gives us more: ash, pebbles, graphite, cobbles-in-the-rain, mother-of-pearl, inside an oyster shell, slate, silver and pewter.

Painted cool grey-and-white stripes in a hall or stairway will never date and will age gracefully. Cool greys all look wonderful with slashes of bright strong colour – bright yellow in particular, but equally jade green, vermilion red or gold. And remember that, in the garden, cool grey plants are valued for their ability to make any flowers of a blue-pink nature look their best. Once again, nature leads the way.

BELOW It takes a brave decorator to use unadulterated black like this, but its effectiveness is beyond question. With the exception of the stripped and varnished wooden boards, all black rules. To use black in these quantities successfully, it is important to contrast finishes and tones. Nothing here is actually the same colour. The rough black of the fireplace is different from the polished black of the chair. The dark blue-grey of the walls differs from that of the heavy, beaten early twentieth-century metal screen. The different materials present in the room, and the subsequent startling difference in textures, are vital to the room's success.

RIGHT In this bedroom, blacks and greys tell a far more muted story. Against a pale-grey wall is a headboard of a soft brown-grey textile, and on white bed-linen are chunky grey knitted cushions. The corresponding furniture is dark wood – very simple, very masculine, but not at all strident.

BLACKS

In the decoration of the Middle Ages, black was much used in the form of judiciously placed fine lines, accentuating the richness of a neighbouring colour. Again, in the early nineteenth century, it was paired with yellow, buff or cream to emphasize and strengthen those colours. Black is, in fact, the squeeze of lemon that brings out the flavour of colours it is paired with.

In some periods, however – notably the Palladian decorative schemes of the early eighteenth century – black was used with more confidence. And in the twentieth century – in what is for me one of the most striking descriptions ever of a fictional room – Dorothy Sayers described the study of her dashing detective, Lord Peter Wimsey, as being decorated in Chinese yellow and glossy black – a dashing combination and one that must have been seen in the rooms of Lord Peter's Regency ancestors.

Black is, of course, associated with night and the dark, as well as with the bachelor flats of would-be Lotharios, which makes it a difficult colour for many people to use. But do not dismiss it; black has many depths. Originally, black pigments were derived from different sources; there was lampblack, bone black (a brown-black) and vine black (a blue-black), and today you can approximate these different tones with paints or tinted glazes, depending on the look you want. Each of these shades can be used to throw other colours and finishes into relief – think of glossy black and rich chestnut, chalky black and warm white, or even the Wimsey way – with bright, reflective yellow.

THIS PAGE In a serious games room, black is the perfect background – a dark cave, and one in which there can be no distraction from the total concentration needed for a game. Here, against a relatively soft grey-black wall, free-standing white columns provide an element of contrast – both in their colour and in their texture – with peeling old white paint which reveals primered grey wood beneath. Japanese-style stools – black, with wicker and wooden seats – stand against the wall, and the pool table itself, although not black, is suitably monumental and more than holds its own in the gloom. Many pieces of furniture would be swallowed up by such dark walls.

Creams and browns

The neutral range continues into the warmer spectrum with creams and browns. Browns – earth tones – are literally the most natural of all colours, for it was in the earth that the search for colour was first undertaken. Words like 'sienna', 'ochre', 'umber' – these are evocative names. And, from dark chocolate brown to yellowy cream, these are colours to which we respond naturally and warmly. Once again, you make a great mistake if you dismiss these tones as dull or bland. As we have seen, well-chosen neutrals can look more expensive than any other group of colours – think 1950s Hollywood star with skin of porcelain and hair of platinum, dressed in sheer nylons, pale cashmere and buttery camel. Neutrals are words like 'putty', 'parchment', 'clotted cream', 'palomino', 'ivory'. They even sound expensive.

Creams

THE VERY WORD 'CREAM' CONJURES UP, FOR GOURMANDS AT ANY RATE, AN IMMEDIATE AND PLEASURABLE ASSOCIATION. RICHER OR PALER, CREAMS ARE FOREVER USEFUL IN THE HOME AND CAN BE USED WHEREVER A TOUCH OF WARMTH IS REQUIRED.

The earth tones of sienna, ochre and umber are just as important today in decorative terms as they were when the artists of antiquity first ground them into powder form and mixed them with mediums to use as paint. When these earth pigments are heated they, not surprisingly, become burnt – giving us yet more evocative names and an almost infinite variety of rich tones that can add warmth, depth or even a cool cast when mixed with other colours. It is, indeed, through the judicious use of these earthy pigments that we can achieve all those tones of cream that the lover of neutrals is so keen to employ.

An entire room, painted in a single shade of cream, would look boring rather than subtle. Indeed, one of the problems that many people find with using cream today in decoration is that it carries

TOP LEFT Cream-painted kitchens are, for many people, reminiscent of the 1930s, the days before fitted kitchens were as ubiquitous – and, in some cases, forbidding – as they are today. In this kitchen of a Manhattan apartment, the cream tiles and units make for a comfortable, even cosy, look with intimations of home-cooking and comfort food. Cleverly, all the china has been chosen to work with the palette, rather than to contrast.

ABOVE AND TOP RIGHT In a small bathroom in the same apartment as the kitchen, a creamy shade of tile – the colour of hot milk and honey – has been contrasted with white for an up-to-the-minute effect. Remarkably easy to achieve, and as smart as the proverbial paint, it is an easy way to treat a bathroom with all-white, period fittings that will neither date nor pall.

A confident and comfortable effect is achieved in this double-height room of neutral shades, where the black of the metal window frames is the only contrast, and no flashes of bright colour have been used. The different tones have been handled with skill – the pale cream of the walls is offset by the warmer tones of the sofa and chair, as well as by the stripped and polished floorboards.

with it an in-built prejudice. For so long during the twentieth century, creams seemed to be thought of as a fail-safe solution, used in situations where the dull was to be preferred. Cream used to carry the stigma of 'good taste', to be used anywhere and everywhere on the grounds that it could never be criticized. There was never any idea of using more than one cream; indeed, one wonders if painters knew there *was* more than one cream.

It is the case, however, that neutrals in general (and creams in particular) always look better when mixed together. Tonal contrast – perhaps on the woodwork or floor and in the textiles – will help to pull the room together and give the scheme depth.

THIS PAGE In this open living space, neutral shades have been used in both deep and pale versions to create warm contrasts. The fireplace wall is thrown into relief by being coloured a pale, rough oatmeal, whilst the remainder of the wall is a deeper, but toning, hessian shade.

Throughout the room there is this contrast of neutral tone: a free-standing structural pillar is matched to the fireplace; the flooring is of pale-cream marble; whilst the open staircase is of simple polished wooden treads that add yet another dimension to the neutral palette.

If, on the other hand, you do not want to employ a full palette of creams in the room you are decorating, it is important to include a note of perceptible contrast. In fact, many decorators feel that any colour on its own – particularly one as subtle as cream – is meaningless *unless* it is combined with at least one other colour. It is, after all, the interdependence of colours and their relationships when presented together that produce successful and harmonic schemes that are pleasing to the eye. Think of a flash of burnt orange, a stripe of leaf green, a slash of pillar-box red; it is combinations like these that add excitement, and they are very easy to achieve within a cream colour scheme. With this in mind, cream – in all its many manifestations – should actually be thought of as the most useful colour in the entire decorating palette. It complements and contrasts with so many other favoured colours and, by slightly adjusting the degree of warmth, it can be used to accentuate, diminish, enhance or dilute.

THIS PAGE In a bedroom, the tone is of warm flesh pink-beige tinted with white. Flat, almost chalky in appearance, it makes a perfect background colour for antique furnishings, as well as being an eminently suitable colour for a room associated with rest and relaxation. On the chest of drawers, a collection of feathers draws attention to the brown undertones of the wall behind.

creams and browns **45**

THIS PAGE Deep chocolate-brown paint, with a glowing silk finish – like the best sort of chocolate bar – is used throughout this room to the most dramatic effect. The curved-back bed has been upholstered in wide-brown-striped cotton and then dressed in an antique patchwork quilt, unusually made from scraps of brown material. Even the wooden floor has been stained, polished and left in its pristine state. With so much strong colour, the window surrounds have sensibly been painted white, and white shutters have been hung instead of curtains. It is difficult to overemphasize how important the touches of white are in this setting.

Browns

SO WIDE IS THE RANGE OF BROWNS, SO SOFT AND WARM, SHARP AND COOL, THAT THEY DEMAND TO BE LOOKED AT WITH A WIDER EYE. NOT ONLY DO THEY WORK WELL WITH MANY OTHER COLOURS, BUT ALSO IN COMBINATION WITH EACH OTHER, PARTICULARLY WHEN TONES SPANNING THE ENTIRE RANGE ARE CHOSEN.

As a popular decorating colour, brown has been somewhat out of favour in recent years. It was much loved in the nineteenth and early twentieth centuries when, in its darkest form, it was widely used on all woodwork and floors, often in a high-gloss finish. Later, in the 1960s, it enjoyed an enthusiastic revival; it sometimes felt as though no room was complete without a single chocolate-brown wall, which often seemed to be complemented by a second wall coloured in a brilliant flame orange.

However, shiny dark brown (much like cold, pale green) was also for a long time associated with cheerless institutions, such as schools, hospitals and government buildings.

WARM BROWNS

We warm to browns, and we particularly warm to warm browns. They make up a wonderful colour group, linked to the natural world, which is probably why we feel such an affinity with them. Think of nuts – pale hazels and polished pecans; of hide – tanned leather and butter-soft suede; of wood – polished maple and pine; of warm spices like cinnamon and nutmeg; and of beans like coffee and cocoa – chocoholics need look no further.

To get the best from warm browns, visualize autumn in its beauty. Perhaps more than at any other time of year, it is in autumn that we remark on the colour of the surrounding landscape, and of deciduous trees in particular. We notice how, as the leaves change and the sun gets lower on the horizon, there is a harmony of tone which crosses the spectrum, ranging from bright yellow-orange browns, to warm, deep red-browns. And, as the leaves

THIS PAGE A decorative scheme that demonstrates again the advisability of leavening all-brown colour schemes with a dash of sharp contrast. In this contemporary, rather masculine dining room, red is the accent colour, on show here in the red leather dining chairs. The brightness of the shade brings into focus the walls, which are the colour of Cuban tobacco leaves, as well as the wooden dining table and the polished parquet floor. A rug of abstract design re-emphasizes the colour scheme.

BELOW Tones of brown, particularly warm browns, are very effective in a bathroom, always making it look warm and comfortable. The secret, with these softer, paler shades – unlike their darker, deeper cousins – is not to stray too far from the milky taupe palette. The whole room is pulled together here by the deeper-toned skirting board.

start to fall, their tints become paler and softer, with a pink tone to them rather than the more strident red.

Warm browns work well together and have always been used to harmonize with other colours. Brown terracotta – not orange and not red – is a fine colour, and like all the red-browns can be very successfully paired with black. A warm reddish brown was particularly popular during the American Colonial period and blended well with wooden floors and polished furniture. These browns are welcoming and can be used to effect in halls and other spaces which need to have an instant effect. Think of tan – tanned leather rather than skin – which is an accommodating shade, neither masculine nor feminine, and which can be used effectively in rooms with neutral functions, such as halls, studies, cloakrooms and bathrooms, as well as an accent in rooms decorated in warm whites. Warm browns are also good for rooms with a cool light, adding comfort and an air of relaxation.

COOL BROWNS

Cool browns are tinged with green, green-yellow or a touch of black. Like warm browns, they are also very much colours of nature – not so much autumnal nature, more nature's background – of tree bark and

The decorative touches in this taupe-toned bathroom come from the functional and the essential. The interest is in the wood-framed mirror, the chrome fittings, the wall-hung towel rail, the towels themselves and even the strip light, hung vertically instead of in conventional fashion. No other details are required.

LEFT AND BELOW Small rooms often look more effective when decorated in a way that emphasizes their cosy qualities. Textile-hung walls always make for instant cocoons, and in this small cloakroom, textured silk – of a surprisingly wide stripe – has been used in nutty tones like hazel and pecan. The second surprise is that the silk has been hung horizontally rather than vertically, which would have been the more obvious choice. In contrast, the floor is of cool-veined cream marble, and the basin is glass; they are balanced by the warmth of the silk.

of dying leaves. Cool browns are camouflage colours, the colours of animal fur and pelts – think donkeys and dormice. They are the colour of garden earth, and often have an element of black in them.

This natural aspect of cool browns reminds one of basic military camouflage colours – often a mixture of cool green, black and cool brown – which are used together because they tend to merge gently into a natural background. Cool browns and cool greens have the power of making objects recede and become subordinate, as well as darkening a room and therefore making it seem smaller. So, when you use these tones, remember that unless you use them with colour or objects that lift them,

THIS PAGE Traditional in one sense, extremely modern and sophisticated in another, the combination of brown and black is very effective when it is handled with confidence. Think of the tall leather boots of Regency Bucks and of Cavalier King Charles spaniels! Nothing could be less dog-like, of course, than this Manhattan living room: it is extremely disciplined, from the choice and placing of the furniture to the way the neutral, but strong, palette is employed.

your scheme, too, will become a background, and perhaps even fade away. Some cool browns are very close to cool greens in tonality, and it is difficult to quantify the colour all the time. A bit more green and it becomes green, a bit more brown and it becomes brown. So many interesting colours come somewhere into this range, such as a colour which is presently popular in some hand-mixed paint ranges; a sort of brown-green putty colour, that sometimes looks as though it has been mixed with a bit of sand or green mud. Cool brown colours, ranging from the pale to the deep, were much used in the beginning of the eighteenth century when they were given names like 'stone' and 'wainscot', describing the surfaces they were imitating.

ABOVE AND BELOW Throughout this room, the sternest discipline is employed to achieve the final effect. The furniture is carefully chosen: a deep-brown leather chair with matching ottoman, and a long cream-and-brown upholstered sofa by Cappellini. The floor is old parquet, rejuvenated in glossy black lacquer. The walls are severe panels: black alternating with pale taupe, and each edged – a telling detail – in chrome. The tables, too, alternate in tone – one in cream-veined marble, the other in shiny glass. Light relief comes from a cappuccino-and-cream rug.

LEFT As in so many contemporary city interiors, the windows are left uncurtained and, here, in their square symmetry, echo the internal design of the room.

Reds, pinks and purples

In their brightest and clearest forms, red, pink and purple are colours to treat with respect, for they demand attention. All shades of red are stimulating and appear in many guises, often edging towards the purple or the pink. Consider some of the natural variations – flowers like hibiscus, camellia or indeed the depth of a red rose. Then think of crimson, claret, coral, carmine and magenta – all assertive and strong. All pinks, of course, are based on red, the dominant primary colour, which has been diluted with white and perhaps a little blue or yellow. Purple, in its strongest form, is a straight combination of red with blue, another primary; and, depending on the strengths and proportions of the two primaries, the resultant purple will be warmer or cooler in tone.

Reds

A RED ROSE IS THE TRADITIONAL SYMBOL OF TRUE LOVE,
YET 'TO SEE RED' IS TO LOSE CONTROL. IT IS EVIDENT
THAT RED, IN ALL ITS MANIFESTATIONS, IS A VERY
POWERFUL COLOUR THAT EVOKES STRONG FEELINGS.

Every culture incorporates red in some guise into
its design and decoration. It is a positive colour,
a colour of life. But that same red has also, even if
subconsciously, more violent associations, such as
those connected with blood, wounds and therefore
battle, with passion and anger. Red is the colour of
revolution, and it can, indeed (if used in undiluted
form) cause revolution in a room.

Red ochre, an earth pigment, was one of the first
sources of red. Another was cinnabar, a naturally
occurring, rare and therefore expensive vermilion. In
China, vermilion was the Imperial red, and so popular
was this strong, assertive pigment that, by the
thirteenth century, it had been produced by chemical
means and was thereafter used widely.

As a pure primary colour, red becomes varied
when it is mixed with other tones in smaller or larger
degrees. As a colour in decorating, red has weight.
It asks to be noticed, and noticed it is. If you do not
want to use it as the dominant colour, just a touch
of red will complete many other colour schemes – it

THIS PAGE Warm, strong and
immensely livable, the walls in
the sitting room of designer
Pascale Bredillet-Boateng are as
much of a red statement as you
could find, and all the better for
that. The walls have been painted
in a matt red pigment and then
glazed over in dark red, so that
a flat effect is avoided. The
purple leather chair and the
brighter, red suede cushions lift
the room without jarring contrast.
The curtains are based still on
red, but lightened with a soft glint
of gold that is echoed in the
cushions on the sofa.

THIS PAGE In Roberto Bergero's apartment in Paris, the walls of the drawing room are matt, flat, uncompromising brick red, but lifted into another sphere by the moulding of the panels which has been subtly picked out in a dragged dark burgundy. The furniture echoes the tones of the walls – a sofa upholstered in dark burgundy velvet, furnished with lustrous velvet cushions; a companion chair is covered in a brighter red silk, and the only dissonant (but important) note, is a golden rod yellow vase, which stands on a grey painted pedestal.

Reds used together in a room can be strident or soft, peaceful or powerful. Combine them with care, making sure that the other colours add light and airiness to the scheme.

Rules – particularly decorative ones – are made to be broken, and the rule book that says strong colours should always have an accent of a contrasting colour has here been thrown away in triumph. Red on red, on red; a deep red leather chair is put against uncompromising matt red cupboard doors – behind which lurk the television and associated equipment. Even the side table is finished in a glossy red stain. A touch of contrast is present in the two paintings, but they are overshadowed by the sheer weight of colour.

has a way of sharpening what might otherwise sink into obscurity. It does this most successfully, of course, with the colour immediately opposite it on the colour wheel – its complementary colour, green – although it should be a tone or shade of green rather than a very strong green. The eye can only take in so much, and two fierce bright tones would be too much.

WARM REDS

There is nothing warmer than a deep, warm red, associated as it is with sensuality and seduction, but also with feelings of comfort and safety. Warm red, particularly as it moves towards the brown, is very successfully paired with white, particularly a creamy, broken white.

Red of a brownish hue can be remarkable successful in a sitting room or a bedroom – think of Tuscan, warm-weather red; think of the deep brown-red of old velvet. This is a shade that has affinities in red, in brown, in black, and can be well used with any of these colours.

Warm red is traditionally thought to be a good colour for a room in which eating takes place, and it is true that its air of warmth adds a sense of relaxation, which is conducive to the enjoyment of food. But, if eating is not confined to a separate dining room, red may be too overpowering. If this is the case, combine the red with less stressful

colours or ensure that the shade you use is not oppressive, perhaps moving towards that vastly underrated colour, geranium.

These warm reds, applied in a flat matt finish, are very effective on woodwork – as it was used, both inside and out, in American Colonial architecture and decoration. (Almost any colour looks good on woodwork, especially skirting, where it can be used to highlight and contrast with the wall colour, or can be painted in the same colour to blend harmoniously with the walls. Woodwork is an area of many homes where so much more imagination could be employed.)

BELOW A room which is pure, condensed colour such as this must rely on changes of texture to give interest and relieve the eye. A sofa covered in warm red velvet is a comfortable foil to the uncompromising sheen of the leather furniture that surrounds it.

TOP RIGHT Another view of this red television room shows how carefully the scale and proportions of the room have been planned. The bookcase and the sofa are exactly the same width, and the height of the bookcase is in perfect proportion to that of the seating below. The pair of tall reading lights add to the perfectly balanced effect, and the red leather ottoman connects with the leather chairs opposite.

RIGHT For many centuries, red was the colour of choice for textile-hung rooms in large houses, particular in eating rooms and for walls where pictures were to be hung. In this bedroom, the wall covering is perhaps simpler than those of the seventeenth century, but none the less effective. These cupboards have been built into the wall and then covered with material – a simple solution to what could be a boring, utilitarian piece of furniture.

When using red and green, choose a subtle olive or drab green. Two bright tones will not accentuate each other; rather, they will murder each other.

LEFT Red shades and tones are particularly effective as woven textiles. This soft fabric, with a light twill effect, is hung throughout the bedroom. Warm and soft, it has been paired with woodwork painted in a flat cream-green – quite similar to the useful eighteenth-century colour known as 'drab'. The carpet is ochre with a hint of green, and the bed-cover is a cheerful, bright-red stitched quilt, which lifts the whole, clever scheme. Caramel-and-white cushions link the bed with the painting in tones of brown and white above.

RIGHT AND FAR RIGHT A period dining room, with dado-height panelling of polished wood and wooden mantelpiece to match, has been coloured in a warm terracotta with a glowing, not glossy finish. Red terracotta, with its underlying brown tones, is perfect in a room filled with wooden furniture. The olive-green glazed fireplace tiles, very much of their time, might, in another setting, look less than totally attractive, but here act as a striking and pleasing counterpoint to the red walls.

COOL REDS

Generally speaking, a cool shade of a colour will harmonize best with other tones in a similar vein. Crimson, a deep rich red inclining towards purple, was one of the most expensive of dyes in early times and therefore associated with rank, as seen in the robes of cardinals and bishops. This deep, regal blue-red harmonizes with blue-green, blue or lilac. Combined with a broken white and a splash of black or grey, it is sophisticated in the extreme. Crimson also works very well with a drab olive green or, indeed, with a flash of purple. Blue-red is not a childish colour and is for use in a grown-up context only.

Somewhat easier to use are the wine reds. Deep claret is traditionally a colour used to convey comfort both of surroundings and life, calling to mind all those deep-claret Victorian velvet-covered library sofas and chairs still to be found. There is something supremely relaxing about the depth of this colour. A deep wine like this looks wonderful with a paler blue-pink, but is less successful with an actual blue, as the overall effect could be too cold.

Still red, but moving towards the pink shades, are the berry reds – loganberry and raspberry. They are, it is true, easier to handle than the deeper reds. Like the fruits they are named after, they are wonderful with cream. Experiment with cool reds; you will find that they are easier to use than you might have anticipated.

Pinks

PINK IS, TRADITIONALLY, A FEMININE COLOUR – LITTLE GIRLS PLUMP FOR PINK PARTY DRESSES; OLDER GIRLS THINK IN TERMS OF PINK TO FLATTER THE FACE. AND PINKS CAN BE EQUALLY FLATTERING WHEN USED IN INTERIOR DECORATION, SO LONG AS YOU THINK PRETTY NOT SWEET, BRIGHT NOT SUGARY, PALE NOT BABY.

Pinks can be hot, vibrant, exciting: think of the pinks of India and Mexico. They can be subtle and cool: think of the pinks of eighteenth-century interiors. In the natural world, pinks can be interesting, evanescent, fleeting – many pink flowers even change their tone, from bright to pale, over the course of the day. Pink, in nature, always looks its best when it is backed by another colour – a herbaceous border composed entirely of pink flowers has no weight and little beauty. It requires the contrast of another shade – preferably plants in tones of grey, silver or olive green – to bring out its subtlety and depth.

Although pinks can be very effective used as the dominant colour in a scheme, they can also add a note of restraint and subtlety to a room. Antique textiles, for example, that were once bright pink often fade to a particularly pleasing soft grey-pink, and it is worth looking out for old textiles or cushions to use in a scheme of rather stronger tones.

Traditional chintz designs very often incorporate a particular blue-pink tone combined with a lavender or pale blue, perhaps in a flower pattern. These sorts of colours used together are particularly interesting on a white or cream background; they result in making the neutral shade appear somehow fresher and cleaner. The same effect – a group of light, cool pinks mixed with white-white or cream – can be used to effect on a larger scale throughout a room. A dash – just a dash – of a sharp strong colour in the same spectrum – dark blue, perhaps – will help to anchor such a subtle scheme.

TOP The view from the dining room of designer Geraldine Prieur's Paris apartment reveals a symphony of pink continuing through the hallway beyond. Walls are washed in shades of pink, with broad stripes of palest summer melon.

ABOVE Throughout the apartment, shades of orange and subtle gilding provide clever contrast. A gold-and-crystal floor light, designed by Geraldine Prieur, looks dashing against a panelled pink wall and bright curtains.

ABOVE The pinks are all slightly different, yet all from the same palette. In the drawing room, the walls are three different pinks; the curtains another, brighter shade; the rug is slightly deeper, with a paler-toned border and a design in dark aubergine scattered across the field. An antique chaise longue has been covered in dull pink material with aubergine and gold stripes. **RIGHT** A red ceramic pot sits on a self-patterned sari-like cloth. Pink tones and gilding provide the link.

In this city kitchen designed by Hugh Broughton, the brightest of brights work together in surprising harmony. Dominating everything else in the room are the kitchen units — where both eye-level cupboards and base units are in the most vibrant pink. The strength of the colour is tempered, however, first by the brushed stainless-steel panels behind the units and over the work surfaces, and secondly by the wide band of white which surrounds the wall of units and continues down to floor level. This white surround might seem a small and insignificant detail, but it is visually very important; it contains the colour almost as if it were in a frame, providing reference and relief to the eye. There are moulded plastic chairs in the same pink as the units, as well as in an equally bright blue and a clear lime green. The blue and green act as accents within the total picture. These are fluorescent colours and, bright as they are, they all have an underlying similarity, in that blue is behind the whole scheme and in every colour — the magenta pink, the yellowy-green, even the stainless steel. More than that, blue, as seen in the industrial rubber floor, is used to link and ground every part of the room.

WARM PINKS

Although warm pinks are soft, all pinks can appear a little cold in a dark or cool room. They work best either when they are used in a broad spectrum of the reds and pinks or mixed with some cream. They can also work when they have a stronger colour to throw them into relief: warm pink and apple green is an uplifting duet, particularly with a little warm white mixed in there somewhere. Warm pinks invite and flatter. They rarely work used on their own – a comment which could be made about many colours but which particularly applies to these pinks. Warm pink is pleasing in a kitchen, where it can give a feeling of

purposeful pleasure or in a small bathroom, adding to the feeling of indulgence and relaxation that every bathroom should have.

One of the most popular of warm pinks is the deep warm hue that veers towards a true terracotta. Think of geranium mixed with brick dust; it is a welcoming, easy-to-live-with colour that will work as well in a room used for eating as in a bedroom. Particularly appropriate and successful in cool lights, it looks wonderful contrasted with buttery cream or with dark, sharp forest green. A similar and equally useful shade is the chalky pale pink of fresh plaster. This is a wonderful colour for walls, acting as a soft

background for greens of every description and also for much stronger pinks, even shocking pink.

Another successful shade of warm pink is apricot, which has slid quietly out of favour over the last few years, and yet has the ability to bring life to any room, to add sunshine to the darkest and dingiest aspect. Perhaps it went out of favour because it was flavoured with either too much yellow or too much pink; the most successful apricot is one where neither shade predominates. If you study a real fruit, there are often at least three different shades that blush its skin – a little pink, a touch of red even, and (usually) a warm yellow.

Gold is a wonderful foil for apricot, bringing out, as it does, the warmth of the tone. Touches of gold could be introduced in the form of a gilded

Pinks bounce colour straight back off the walls and make all the surfaces around them glow with a hint of pink.

THIS PAGE An Art Deco bed, with a bedhead of rich walnut veneer and its matching bedside table, is the starting point for this rich, yet soft bedroom, belonging to designer Pascale Bredillet-Boateng. Tone is what this bedroom is all about – behind the bed is a vibrant pink hanging, at the window is a sheer curtain of a softer pink, and on the bed is a bedspread of palest powder pink. Everything is lifted and pulled together by the fuchsia-pink and fudge-brown suede cushions.

frame around a picture or mirror or it might simply be a judicious, fine line along a dado rail or around a window. Gold tones are also, of course, perfect against any pink, warm or cool. Gold adds an air of sybaritic luxury, and can be employed not just as leaf or paint but also as a heavier metal – brass, perhaps, in the guise of heavy curtain poles against a warm pink wall.

OPPOSITE This bedroom is a quiet retreat of diluted and softened colours. The walls are painted white, and the floor – which is laid throughout the apartment, and unifies the different areas – is powder-blue rubber with a high sheen to it. The main storage is in a pale pink curved wardrobe on one side of the room. A black iron bedhead sits behind a simple bed, which is made up with white bed-linen and pale-pink cushions.

COOL PINKS

Cool pink is perhaps the most sophisticated colour in this spectrum, its blue or grey tones giving it a striking subtlety. It is a very flattering colour to live with, always useful, like the perfect blusher in a make-up box. Think dusty, dusky old rose pinks, mixed with – or set against – yellow, grey, blue, sage, olive green or deep blue-red. These are shades that look particularly effective with warm browns of a chestnut hue. Strong cool pinks are very dramatic and work well when used to highlight or point out other

decorative features. Indeed, these tones can be so dramatic that, when used as the dominant colour, a strong cool pink can quite simply be too much, veering towards the strident.

If you are unsure, a little will go a long way: think of the bright, cold pink of a cushion made in Thai or Indian silk. It has an immediate effect on the dowdiest of sofas or chairs. If you are confident in what you are doing, then by all means combine strong pink with other colours of equal weight – deep mauve, citrus yellow, artificial grass green or even electric

BELOW In this drawing room, a pink palette has been used, but with the emphasis on brown tones rather than blue. The walls here are coloured a soft dusty pink – one of the most forgiving and livable with of colours. Against this background, the furnishings are coloured tones that blend in, from pale cream to dark russet-burgundy velvet. The patterned rug – brick, tan and stone – and even the floor cushions (embroidered velvet on a taupe base), blend and harmonize.

blue. But do not use them all together, and certainly do not use them without some respite, which might take the form of a white, cream or another neutral that comes equipped with its own blue note.

There are, as always, horticultural analogies – think of a dianthus or carnation – of cool pink tones, set off with a darker fringing of deep, cool red and surrounded with green-grey or just plain grey leaves. Of course, pink is a wonderful exterior colour, particularly in a distemper finish, which evokes colour-washed, rough-plastered houses, warmed by the sun.

THIS PAGE The curtains in this room of calm are of unlined silk. Bold stripes of ivory, orange and pink add a warm glow to the room as the daylight is filtered through tall windows. The woodwork and ceiling are painted white and it is interesting to see how the pink and gold colours throughout the room are reflected by the white. This is why white should never be considered in isolation but always in tandem with the colours that are to be combined with it.

Purples and lilacs

THE FIRST-CENTURY WRITER PLINY CALLED PURPLE 'THE COLOUR OF HEAVEN' AND, IN ITS RICHNESS, PURPLE HAS ALWAYS BEEN ASSOCIATED WITH ROYALTY. HOWEVER, AS SEEN IN THE LESS INTENSE HUES OF LILAC AND VIOLET, THIS IS ONE OF THE MOST SUBTLE OF COLOURS, DISAPPEARING INTO THE INVISIBLE BANDS OF THE COLOUR SPECTRUM.

It is always important to remind yourself, when thinking about a colour, which primaries that colour is derived from. Purple, of course, derives from red and blue and, depending on the strength of those colours, it can vary enormously, from a brown-purple like sun-faded old velvet, to a rich Imperial blue-purple, like the robe of a Roman emperor.

Purple harmonizes with many colours: yellows, including lemon yellow, citrine and maize; blues, too, both dark and light; and even a pale orange – not an easy combination but one that looks spectacular when carefully combined.

Purples, and particularly their lighter variants, mauves, went through a bad patch in the middle of the nineteenth century, when the development of chemical dyes meant that these colours – along with many other, equally harsh new bright shades – became available to all. They were immediately popular and these new shades were used with ubiquitous enthusiasm on textiles, walls and floors, many of them together in a clashing cacophony. In the twentieth century, poor purple again suffered many of the same indignities: used to excess in the 1960s and 1970s, teamed with unsuitable colours, it unsurprisingly fell from favour. But today it is very much back, not only in its full glory, but also in its softer, subtler, paler variants – mauve and lilac.

Mauve and lilac are true flower colours. Think of sweet peas – pale pink, mauve, lilac and cream, against soft green leaves. These lilac shades are so quiet that they almost fade as you look at them; and then there is the eponymous shrub, sometimes growing into a tree, whose panicles of flowers combine grey-mauve, pale blue and white. And recall the true viola – a little bit of deep-purple velvet, a little soft, bright mauve, and a hint of yellow – look no further for perfection.

THIS PAGE Against the warm purple-washed walls, the panelled wood beneath the dado rail, like the leaves on a bunch of grapes, is coloured a soft, spring-like yellowy green, which works wonderfully with the purple above. The colour theme is continued with the purple cloth on the table and the dining chairs, which are covered in either warm purple or pale-blue velvet. At the end of the room, a deep-burgundy velvet curtain stands in front of an open cupboard, which has been painted French grey. The china and glasses on the table and stacked in the console continue the theme – either in cool glassy green or in the same complementary tones of golden-green as the dado panelling. This is a room for celebration – like the vines it is reminiscent of, it calls to mind bacchanalian revelry.

OPPOSITE So conducive to eating, this dining room in Paris which belongs to master colourist and well-known designer, Michelle Halard, rejoices in its rich-coloured walls. The surfaces have been coloured with a base coat of lilac, washed over with a stronger tone of the same hue. Gilding and tones of gold are everywhere in the room, combining with golden-green accents to accentuate the warm plum tones. A soft grey-green console is home for an assortment of plates and further complements the colour scheme.

This London apartment designed by Gordana Mandic and Peter Tyler is layered with colour. Throughout the space, the ceilings are painted pale lilac, in order to provide a more gentle contrast than white to the strong colours on the walls and furnishings.

RIGHT AND BELOW The bedroom is painted a quiet shade of pale lilac, both on the walls and the built-in cupboards. The accents of colour come from a side-shelf in deeper purple and bed-linen in sharp fuchsia pink.

CENTRE The living area, which has a dark-wood floor, is coloured in shades of deep purple. The wall colour was achieved by mixing purple pigment into the plaster, which gives it a particularly rich texture. The surface was then coated with a layer of yacht varnish, which gives it a slight sheen and an even greater depth. Purple-covered benches make up a seating area, and a rug of wool patchwork introduces more accent colours, like orange, chrome yellow, grey and biscuit.

WARM PURPLES

At first sight, red-purples are not very easy colours to use in interior decoration, though when they are used well they are instantly appealing and welcoming. Thinking about the colour is perhaps easier if one envisages the aubergine, piled high on market stalls and looking inviting, rich and warm. Bright saffron yellow, grey or white – all these shades can be used to bring warm purples to life. They also look wonderful with silvery greys and grey-green, but they can be difficult to blend together with other purple tones.

Like their close associates, the red-browns, warm purples can make a room feel comfortable and warming, as well as making a large room diminish in size. They are ideal tones for an eating room – inviting relaxation and the enjoyment of food. Perhaps it is the association with the colour of good wine that makes it so suitable. For a truly cocoon-like feeling, use warm purple with deep red and emulate the best

of Victorian decoration – combine several different textures, making sure that the deep luxury of cut, velvet-like pile is included in the mix. Warm purple is a surprisingly good colour for woodwork, particularly when combined with neutral shades.

There are some varieties of lilac which are warm in tone. This is caused by the addition of pink, as can be seen in that coarser acquaintance of the lilac, the buddleia or butterfly bush. A sophisticated way to use these pink lilacs is to mix them with duck-egg blue and grey, with perhaps a flash of a deeper blue shot through the scheme. A warm buttery cream looks wonderful with pink lilacs, too, and they also work well with their aubergine cousins.

ABOVE One of the easiest ways to add slashes and flashes of accent colours to a scheme is with cushions; dependable, often expendable, they can be a good way to experiment with new and clever combinations. They can also be moved around a space at will, depending on where the colour accents are required.

Lilacs and mauves enjoy popularity in every age, and their time in this new century has already arrived.

COOL PURPLES

Lilacs and mauves were much loved and much used at the end of the nineteenth and into the twentieth century. Legendary twentieth-century eccentric, Osbert Sitwell, in the first part of his autobiography, *Left Hand, Right Hand,* describes a house in 1900: 'In the house we had taken, mauve, I remember was the colour on which each scheme was founded. Indeed mauve was the acme of fashion in all branches of decoration, whether for ceilings or wall-papers, and for coverings, of a woman herself no less than of her furniture.' Perhaps as a reaction to all this centennial decorative excitement, lilacs and mauves then fell from favour and for some time seemed to be associated with old ladies – due, doubtless, to the fashion for grey-haired matrons to have a lilac rinse! But these cool tones are in reality sophisticated and clever and, as such, have always had their fans. The French, for instance, never consigned them to purdah, and have always employed them with skill. Greys, deep blues, bright yellows and sage green can all be used with lilacs and mauves. Think also of true lavender – a subtle colour that is not quite grey, not quite blue. Look at a lavender field in bloom, at the waves of colour that fall across it, ranging from an almost blue shade to a grey lilac.

TOP RIGHT AND TOP LEFT Lilac is a soothing shade and therefore one which is good in a room dedicated to work. In this small office there is no obvious distraction: the furniture and woodwork are white and everything else is painted in the same tone of lilac, including the radiator; the only contrast is a pair of distressed green-painted metal chairs. Even the flowerpots look good painted in tones of lilac, hiding glass jars for flowers.
ABOVE From the painted floor to the bed-dressing, this bedroom is like a paint swatch card for lavender blue, running through ever-deepening shades of the palette.

THIS PAGE Is it hyacinth or is it lavender? And does it matter, when the finished effect is this attractive? The mauve-blue colour wash on these walls – actually, blue tones washed over pink – has been used to pull together a group of quite disparate objects that range from a speckled pinky mauve tin to two jasperware-style plaques above the mantelpiece. It is a decorative idea to gather together all the objects you have that are part of the same colour spectrum as a group. The pink tones of the wall colour are brought out and emphasized by the striped seat cushion of the small wooden chair.

Blues: azure to aqua

What colour springs to mind when you think of blue? Is it the cool grey-blue associated with Scandinavia or the rich blue of Greece that seems to reflect the sparkle of the surrounding sea? Or is it the blue of an English spring day – clear and light, neither hot nor cold? The list could go on and on; everyone has their own favourite: for one it is sapphire blue, for another bird's egg blue. Although this wonderful range is, in one sense, charming, in another (more practical) sense it means that it is quite difficult to pick the right shade. Not only does it have to be the shade or tone which you empathize with and warm to personally, it also has to be the right shade for the particular room – which might depend on such practical and diverse factors as which way the room faces, how large it is, and how much sun it gets.

THIS PAGE AND OPPOSITE TOP
Blue can be a surprisingly dramatic colour when used on its own as a background; in this bedroom, the grey-blue wall stands out and makes a fine background. This shade of blue is suited to many things – engravings, a nineteenth-century wooden bed, and an eye-catching dress jacket and matching fez. The clear coral red in the bedspread and also in the jacket is an excellent contrast to the grey-blue of the walls. It is important to gauge the depth of blue required: too bright is overly attention seeking, too pale is to disengage with the needs of interior design.

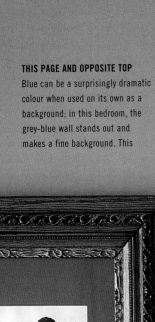

Shades of blue

OF ALL THE COLOURS OF THE SPECTRUM, BLUE IS THE ONE MOST OFTEN CITED AS A FAVOURITE COLOUR. PERHAPS THIS IS BECAUSE OF THE MULTITUDE OF OPTIONS IT OFFERS. NO OTHER COLOUR VARIES SO MUCH IN TERMS OF REFERENCE AND CHOICE, AND WITH SUCH A RANGE AVAILABLE IT WOULD BE HARD NOT TO FIND A BLUE THAT APPEALS TO YOU.

BELOW In this slate-blue room, the artefacts provide the colour – the walls supply the setting. A traditional, painted wooden Indian door frame – or perhaps window frame – is attached to the upper half of the entrance, blending with the colours of the walls: pistachio green and a pale terracotta pink. A sofa, close-covered in a self-patterned gold fabric, has arms upholstered like bolsters, which are reminiscent of Indian nineteenth-century decoration under the Raj.

Blue is not just a modern favourite – historically, the rich variety of blue tones has long been appreciated. Think of Nankeen or Nankin blue, for example, the brilliant deep blue found on the highly collectable blue-and-white Chinese porcelain exported from the Orient in the eighteenth century and which was made from a highly purified salt of cobalt; ditto powder blue, which was originally obtained by blowing powdered cobalt onto the surface of the porcelain.

Blue is a colour of mystery and of subtlety; it is the colour not just of the sky, but also of heaven, and comes clothed with all the many associations of that word. Early painters loved blue and used the fabulously expensive ultramarine wherever money and art allowed. In medieval paintings, because of its cost, it was often used to paint the Madonna's robes, which is why we associate this colour with her today. Medici blue is named after Catherine de Medici, daughter of Lorenzo, who in 1533 married Henry II of France and who brought Italian artists and craftsmen to France to decorate the Tuileries and work at the Luxembourg and Gobelin tapestry factories. Cool Titian blue is the grey-blue of the jacket of Titian's painting, 'Man with a Blue Sleeve', and the coolest of blues is what we now call Wedgwood blue, developed by Josiah Wedgwood in the mid-1700s and widely used on his popular jasperware.

Blue is the colour we think of at the beginning of every day. There can be few of us who do not give a passing glance to the morning sky outside our window, and for most people the bluer the sky, the more cheerful we feel. In the colour spectrum, blue is a colour that appears to recede. Garden designers know this, and often use blue – as they also do white – at the end of a long border in order to give an air of distance and to allow the eye to travel on and beyond. As in horticulture, so in the decoration of our homes: blue used on the walls has the effect of subordinating objects, or making them recede into the background. Interior designers also know that some blues are so strong that they cannot be mixed with anything else, but must stand alone, and that purple-blue flowers look their best mixed with plants with a lemony-green hue – the analogy is obvious and easy.

WARM BLUES

While blues can be the coolest hues of the spectrum, they can also be warm and sunny colours, and a pale blue is not necessarily an icy one. Warm blues have a little pink in them and, on the whole, work better in cooler countries (where they can help to add warmth to the whole room) than they do in sunny, hot climates. Indeed, in a cold room, warm blue can often be combined with a warm pink and cream to create a look reminiscent of a summer sunset, with pink-streaked clouds against the blue sky – think of how the pink-white of the clouds lifts both the blue and the pink of the changing sky.

Bright blues are usually warm; the ancient Chinese – who loved colour – often used a bright, light blue in the decoration of the upper part of their rooms; ceilings were blue (except for Imperial ceilings, which were sacred yellow) and glazed blue tiles covered their roofs. Then there are the clear, rather confident

THIS PAGE In architect Voon Wong's apartment in a converted school in London, blues of different tones are used in the same space to delineate different areas. At the far end of the room, behind a wall-long suede-covered bench, which has been trimmed in orange, the wall is painted a dark blue-grey. At the other end of the apartment, the wall of the entrance hall is painted a clear, strong bright blue, with a decorative and functional alcove, painted in white, cut into the wall. The glossy dark-grey painted wooden floor unites the two tones.

The sunny blues of clear southern skies lift the spirits and bring remembered warmth to colder climates.

Provençal blues, which speak of warm, bright skies, or the colour of a southern sea with the sun shining on it. Blues like these can lift the spirit and are made to bring warmth to colder climates. If you want to make a real statement, pair them with an equally strong yellow, such as gold or egg-yolk yellow, maize or corn. However, a colour combination as strong as this will probably need a mediating dash of a softer colour that harmonizes with both the dominant hues. Warm blues will even work with orange, although not in too great a quantity, and again if you are using an orange that

THIS PAGE In a small London flat, the tiny downstairs shower room has been lined entirely with swimming-pool paint in a bright marine blue. The stainless-steel fittings contrast freshly against the blue, and, to extend the marine analogy, the bathroom window has been designed in the shape of a porthole. Sea blue can be effective in any room, but is especially so when used in a watery setting.

is the same strength as the blue, you may well need another tone added at some point in order to ground the scheme.

One of the warmest of blues is the colour that today we associate with the rippling blue of an inviting swimming pool on a sunny day, or slightly deeper – the Caribbean or Mediterranean sea. In the Caribbean, bright clear blue is often mixed hugger-mugger with a whole range of colours, from bright pinky mauve to clear yellow and bright, light lime green. Very cheerful when you see them in situ, but remember that intense colour has a different effect when it is seen under intense light. Strong light drains all colours of their intensity – strong as well as subtle. Therefore, very bright colour combinations do not look as good in the cold light of more temperate climes – in much the same way as the grass skirt from Hawaii may not have quite the same effect in the local coffee shop as it did in the tropical beach bar! If you are going to translate bright blues into a cooler light, a calmer shade usually works better.

Although we love blue, we can sometimes be frightened by it; it seems so natural and yet, when it is on the wall, it can look so forbidding; it is a very dominant colour, far more dominant than one remembers when looking at a small swatch or colour card. A warm blue springs from the wall with bright alacrity and can make other colours look dirty or dull. This is possibly the main reason why warm clear blues, mixed with creamy white, are perennially popular. The

THIS PAGE In this striking New York kitchen, the work surface and splash-back have been made from an unusual blue marble, which is heavily veined with lapis lazuli. This is the inspiration for the decoration of the room. The wall colour behind is the most wonderful, pure hue, and was chosen to match the darkest veins of the precious mineral in the worktop below. The marble would be striking on its own, but is even more so when teamed with the wall colour. Each surface is strengthened by its proximity to the other. The brushed stainless-steel appliances further complement the colour theme.

combination is forgiving and easy to live with, and can be used in many situations. Blue mixed with white or cream becomes a restful combination and can be well employed where such characteristics are desired – such as in the bedroom, or in a living room or study.

A blue-and-white scheme can also offer a welcome backdrop to other colours. A good way of finding colours that look their best used within this combination is to think of (or even to arrange physically) vases of flowers in different colours against a blue-and-white background. Depending on the exact tone of the blue, almost every shade can be made to look at its best in small doses – a fairly random selection might include dark colours, like crimson and purple; bright colours like jade, mustard and flame; and subtle colours like old rose, sage green and violet.

COOL BLUES

Blues can be so cool and so deep. Blue can be the darkest of hues, as in the deepening blue of the evening sky as it slowly moves towards the darkest blue-black of night. Think mood indigo, songs

LEFT, ABOVE AND ABOVE RIGHT This bedroom, with its walls of powder blue, is very beautiful, but also very cool indeed, as the palette of cool blues moves ever closer to grey. A collection of frosty Venetian glassware sits on the chest of drawers and the bed is made up with snowy-white, intricately ornamented sheets – the coolness of each is emphasized by the uncompromising and all-encompassing colour of the walls.
TOP LEFT AND OPPOSITE A blue as clear and bright as this positively invites an energetic approach to life, as well as making

a luminous background for pictures and objects. In this kitchen, the blue walls are combined with so much white – on the tiles, the woodwork, the appliances and even the floor – that the whole room has an air of freshness and light. The white tiles also act as a perfect backdrop for a collection of blue spongeware kitchen utensils. Flowered tiles in a decorative band – sometimes single depth and sometimes double – mark not only the division between plain tiles and wall but also run around the doorway and down to the floor.

THIS PAGE Grey-blue tones have been employed throughout much of this London apartment, particularly in the bathroom and bedroom. The colours were deliberately chosen to complement the city's naturally soft-grey winter light. The effect, however, is warm rather than foggy. In the bathroom, textures of grey – using materials such as limestone and aluminium – lead to the bedroom beyond, where the painted walls and gloss-painted floor are almost grey, almost blue. The blue-grey pebbles lined up at the edge of the bath remind us that these colours pay homage to the natural world outside.

named after the purple-blue dye extracted from the leaves of the indigo plant and which sum up the feelings behind countless, timeless blues songs. And also think pale, cool, nearly cold, blue. There is the blue of a misty day – a blue which is tinged with grey. There is the blue of wood smoke and of cool grey-blue eyes. Historically, there is Wedgwood blue, a clear blue with a tint of grey. We associate cool blues with the North: ice can be blue, shimmering on a frozen pond or an ice floe; think of the children Gerda and Kay in the ice palace of Hans Christian Andersen's *The Snow Queen*, walking across floors of blue ice and underneath glistening blue stalactites. Actually all those colours we now associate with Scandinavia – often putting them into a general basket of Scandinavian blues – have an element of ice-grey within them.

Cool blues are amongst the most sophisticated tones within the colour spectrum. They are, indeed, soothing and calm and make a wonderful background for a whole range of other colours, from those which

LEFT In this bathroom, the broken blue and white shades of the mosaic wall are softened by the use of clear and opaque plastics. A wall of corrugated clear plastic diffuses the daylight, while the same material, painted, is used to clad the bath. The clear white shower curtain reflects the colours around it, and the overall effect is one of soft, translucent grey-blue, which brings a fresh and welcoming feel to the room.
BELOW Blue mosaic tiles surround a recessed storage area for towels as well as pots and potions; naturally, the towels are also blue.
BOTTOM The plastic-clad bath glows with a softer blue than that of the surrounding mosaics. A sybaritic touch comes with the blue candles.

are its neighbours on the colour wheel, like lime green, turquoise and emerald green, to those which are in contrast, such as dark rich purple, which still has some unseen blue within it.

Cool, pale blues are also very effective used with other light colours in a palette of pastel tones. Think of pale pink, primrose yellow and perhaps even a pale green. A good dollop of cream, and the effect will be of a Neapolitan ice cream. And, if you are using cool blue with white, the white must, of course, be just right – a blue-white, naturally.

Traditionally, cool blues have often been accented with gold – think of seventeenth- and eighteenth-century French interiors, where entire rooms were

decorated in a scheme of light French blue paired with ornamental gilding on plasterwork and wood, the two complementing each other perfectly. Whilst you might not wish today to cover all your plaster with sheets of gold leaf, some fine gold lines outlining panelling, emphasizing moulding or, indeed, painted directly onto blue walls or doors to suggest panels, could be most effective. The gold gives a tone of warmth that is as subtle as the colour it is highlighting.

Note that the adjective that we use to describe these blue tones is 'cool' rather than 'cold'. One is appealing, and the other is to be avoided. It is a question of degree. But then with colour it always is. Because these blues are so close to the tones of winter daylight, it is especially important to try them out first. Test them on the walls and observe them in natural light at all times of day before you commit. You will see that some will look interesting and subtle and some will simply disappear. When you are using an inherently cool colour, texture is even more important than usual. Interestingly, a matt texture gives depth to a cool blue and even a certain warmth. A cool blue in the same shade made up in a gloss finish or a shiny satinized texture – like a pond that has been iced over – immediately becomes that dreaded word – cold.

Scandinavian blue can be cooler than the equivalent grey, making it such a difficult colour to use.

LEFT Shades of cool blue are mixed with white to give a calm, but never dull, look. The strong blue seat cushions and white-painted boards lift the room from the simply soothing to the definitely stylish.
FAR LEFT ABOVE Contrast – an important element when using a single colour – is achieved here by pleating a darker blue-and-white fabric behind the chicken-wire panels of this large cupboard.
FAR LEFT BELOW It is the simplicity of blue that makes it so successful. Around this traditional ceramic sink, a design based on folk-art motifs has been stencilled on a tin splash-back. The painted border looks almost as if it is made of ceramic tiles.
RIGHT A free-standing dresser has been painted blue and wittily finished with gold leaf outlining the door panels – a decorative device usually seen on far grander pieces of furniture. An assortment of blue-and-white china adds to the charm.

Greens: emerald to lime

For most of us, green is the colour we most readily associate with the natural world around us. Just as the blue or blue-grey dome of the sky is over our heads each day, so, too, do we notice green on a daily basis. Albeit unconsciously, nearly everyone, whether they are country or city dwellers, is aware of the greens of nature as they mark the passage of the year. Bright, pale and fresh yellow-greens mean spring is here; darker, deeper greens speak of high summer; while fading, changing greens, becoming ever more muted, take us through autumn and into the long days of winter. The range of greens and their harmonious aspects means that they can be used more widely than almost any other colour of the spectrum. However, this range also means that it is all too easy to choose the wrong green.

Shades of green

PERHAPS JUST BECAUSE GREENS ARE ALL AROUND US IN NATURE, IT IS EASY TO TAKE THEM FOR GRANTED, AND TO ASSUME THAT THEY WILL ALWAYS WORK WHEREVER THEY ARE USED. BUT A COLOUR OF SUCH SUBTLETY NEEDS DECORATIVE CARE AND MUCH THOUGHT.

Green has been a favourite colour since at least the Middle Ages. When we speak of Lincoln green, with its connotations of Robin Hood, we are talking about the dark-green shade which came from the yellow of a particular broom plant mixed with woad or other blue vegetable dyes. Material dyed in this green was the distinguishing mark of the English free archers during the twelfth and thirteenth centuries. And Adam green – or Adam's green as it was originally known – immediately and irrevocably conjures up those light-painted ceilings and stucco patterns inspired by the Greek and Roman ruins visited by Robert Adam during his European journeys in the eighteenth century. Greens were always the most expensive colours in the eighteenth century because many of them were based on expensive bases such as verdigris (green crystals formed on copper) and smalt (cobalt-coloured glass). During that period, all greens, not just Adam green, were particularly popular and were used widely and generously in homes. Throughout the nineteenth century, too, green was used on the walls as well as the woodwork, and was woven into textiles of every description.

Although many of us feel an affinity towards green, both warm and cool greens are in fact rather difficult to use successfully in interior decoration. Green is a very subjective colour and, if the tone is wrong, it can quickly affect our mood.

ABOVE AND RIGHT Michelle Halard is an authoritative French designer who uses colour in a way that shows such confidence and originality that one can only admire and hope to learn from her ideas. In her Parisian apartment, one colour-filled room succeeds another; in the living room, the decorative scheme emanates from the green velvet-coloured walls. Curtains across a doorway are in the same material, so there is no break in the depth of colour around the room. The textural depth and richness of these velvet walls make them a perfect foil for an eclectic assortment of pictures – little wonder that green was the preferred nineteenth-century colour for art-gallery walls.

OPPOSITE Contrasting with the walls, is a mint-green sofa, warm red-brown tall-backed chairs, with painted panels of yellow and blue; and, brightest of all – on a parquet floor painted a very dark brown-black – is a multicoloured rug, combining lilac, blue, yellow, red and white. It is a testimony to owner Michelle Halard's colour sense and the clever way in which she combines tones and hues that there is no jarring note and no sense that the combination of colours is in any way too much.

THIS PAGE This dining room in a late seventeenth-century house which overlooks a fjord outside Bergen in Norway is painted a strong, warm green. The walls are made from horizontally applied planks and the colour dates from the time when the house was built. The green is complemented by seats and cushions in pale olive-and-white checks and stripes, and contrasted with the heavy white door frames. The floor is uncovered – the better to appreciate the warm wood tones – and the green theme continues into the next room with a wide painted band between the ceiling and the picture rail.

WARM GREENS

Warm greens are those with red or yellow tints. Or they are those warm muddy greens mixed from brown-yellow which has been added to blue. It is these combinations that give those satisfying warm greens that work so well set against other colours with yellow in them, such as a sharp orange or, indeed, yellow itself.

These warm greens are the colour of nature, of the warm earth and the woodland. Such earth greens are akin to earth browns and look good combined with all other browns, from chocolate to chestnut and even terracotta. Perhaps because of their historical popularity, warm greens can be quite formal in

character. Objects and pictures are well displayed against a warm green background – a fact that explains the number of galleries and museums that use warm-green paint or materials on the walls; in the late nineteenth century, aesthetic souls advocated dull, dark warm green as the only possible background for works of art.

A slightly redder dark green – Forest or Racing Green, in paint-card terms – is a good colour with which to present an instant air of sophistication and masculinity. Traditionally, this is the colour of studies, libraries and billiard rooms and it is best combined with shiny black – perhaps on dado rails and skirting boards – and with the warm brown of seasoned,

BELOW LEFT The door, door frame and banisters have been painted a slightly darker shade than the floor of this hallway. The horizontally planked walls are a wonderful soft, old pink – another authentic period colour and one that looks absolutely perfect with the deep yellow-green.
BELOW You do not need a wide colour range to create differing and attractive colour schemes. Here, green has been used on the floor and paired with dusty white-painted planks. The earth-toned, red-painted bench is an important part of this harmonious trio, completing the simple but cleverly conceived scheme.

Perhaps no other colour presents so many variations on a theme as green; on its own, combined or contrasted with other colours, its decorative applications are infinite.

THIS PAGE AND OPPOSITE This drawing room in a landmark building in Manhattan is painted in a bold blue-olive green, the sort of colour that might have been used in early eighteenth-century houses. The colour is so strong and so rich that no effort has been made to aggrandize it by adding ornament or contrast to the mouldings or woodwork. Everything seen against this colour, from pictures to furniture, looks the better for it. The blue side of the palette has been complemented by the claret and blue tones of the Oriental rug, and emphasized by the wide claret-and-white stripes of the antique sofa.

leather armchairs and polished mahogany doors. Warm greens also work well – often spectacularly well – with warm reds. These are complementary tones, of course, and a dash (no more) of one in a scheme of the other will always be successful.

Another group of warm greens have an air about them, a feeling of what can only be described as jollity. They call to mind the Emerald isle, the precious stone, and the green of hand-rolled, striped summer lawns. This is what a warm green should be – positive and confident. Jade green also comes into this category, clear and warm, intensely sophisticated and very dominating. Use these colours carefully – in dining rooms perhaps, or hallways and staircases. Consider what colour woodwork to have with these bright colours – the conventional answers are not always best; think instead of a contrast or a deeper tone of the same colour.

COOL GREENS

Greens are popular today as interior-decorating colours, but in the eighteenth and nineteenth centuries they were wildly popular, and used throughout the home, inside and out. Inside the house, the walls were sometimes a pale cool green, or a pale grey-olive, and sometimes a deeper tone, a true deep olive with a hint of grey in it. There was also a lot of the muddy greyish yellow-green, known as 'drab', that was used on woodwork and in more functional areas of the house. There is a shade available today which is similar to traditional drab, but slightly softer and greyer in tone, and – for me – this colour works in every area where once you might have used white or cream: on doors, window frames and shutters, for example. It is best applied in a matt or silk finish and I even use it on

the sort of wooden furniture that needs to be painted. It is never intrusive – it is actually far less intrusive than white as it melts into the background. It is, in fact, a very accommodating colour.

Out of doors, in the eighteenth century, a very dark black-green was often used, both on the exterior woodwork and also on the ironwork of a house, instead of the rather boring black so universally used today. Black ironwork only became fashionable in Britain during Queen Victoria's extended mourning period for her husband, Prince Albert. This shift in opinion led people to opine that green should never be used as an external colour as it was very likely to clash with those many greens that nature delivered so much better. But actually, a cool grey-green, whether dark or light, works very well against a natural backdrop, as indeed, does that once-fashionable dark, Victorian green. The secret is to avoid clear or bright green – the sort of green that children's toys are painted with. Any tone that looks as if it is trying to vie with nature could only ever come off second-best.

ABOVE A pale spearmint green with a touch of soft cream makes this one of the most difficult of colours to achieve – a warm, light green. The warmth is underlined by the wood-framed mirror and the soft green tiles over-glazed with cream.
LEFT The best place to learn about pale, warm greens is outside, where they are at their best and softest, be it as painted, weathered wood or as the natural, almost silvery tones of lichen on a piece of bark.

Dark green absorbs light and, the more black there is within the green, the more light it absorbs, so it should be used with care. That said, a really dark black-green is a very useful colour, decoratively speaking; thought of as a predominantly French colour, it really does look like black, flecked with dark-green lights. It is sometimes called invisible green and is very effective and

sophisticated on a glossy front door, or used inside on skirtings and round door and window frames.

For many people, the cool greens that are easiest to use are those with grey in them: think of the leaves of ivy and myrtle, olive, sage and willow. Garden designers often balance a garden that has too much pink in it by using liberal plantings of grey-green

THIS PAGE In the Paris apartment of designer Michelle Halard, the kitchen exudes an air of tranquillity as well as efficiency. It is painted in the softest, most attractive, shade of sage green. The walls, doors, windows and even the panelling below the dado are all painted in the same shade, which adds to the air of calm. Set against the glossy black-painted parquet floor and behind the black-painted shelves and table, the

combination is at once both sophisticated and eminently easy to live with. The kitchen leads directly into a stunning, strongly coloured purple-and-lilac dining room (see pages 68–9) with which the grey-green is in perfect harmony. A zinc work surface, plus the glassware and steel utensils on show, continue the cool tone, while, behind the working area of the kitchen, the walls are clad with warming wood.

In an Italian city apartment, a bold scheme has been executed in the bedroom. The walls have been washed with a strong, although light, green which is a cross between the bark of an olive tree and the green of its leaves. The wall behind the bed has been framed with a wide band of wash in a more intense shade of the same colour; a narrow band of white separates the two tones. The perfect tone of red toile de jouy – warm and with a little brown in it – has been used with this interesting green (red being green's complementary colour). The effect is positively inviting.

or silver-leafed plants; they also make full use of grey-green plants in borders of gardens which are predominantly white – the grey-green tones soften the white and give it a subtlety and depth that it would otherwise lack. Both these horticultural ideas can be well employed inside the house as well. Think of how well grey-greens would work in a scheme that included blue-red or hot pink tones. And a room of neutral whites would benefit enormously from the addition of pale grey-greens. As with so many colours, it is the subtlety of shade that counts, as well as the subtlety of contrast.

Other cool green hues include the yellow-greens; to identify these greens, think of the natural world in spring, when so many new, young yellow-greens vie for our attention. Think apple, lime, young box and daffodil stems. And, in the vegetable basket, think of fresh green salad leaves: lettuce, celery and the acid green of young radish leaves. For me, these yellow-greens, fresh as they are, look best combined with other clear bright colours, such as yellow and sharp pink. White – or, better still, cream – is important when you are combining these tones. In fact, in some cases it is an essential ingredient, as too many fresh colours can tumble and knock each other over, each shouting to be recognized.

As already observed, greens can quickly swing from the calming to the depressing. When used in the wrong way, they can make one think in particular of all those institutional acres of public areas that surround us. Eau de nil, for example, a colour which was very popular at the beginning of the twentieth century, and which has

RIGHT A clever three-dimensional illusion – like a picture frame or an open book – has been given to this room by running the wide band of washed green on both sides of the inner edges of the wall, edging it with white on either side. It looks like a piece of antique French ribbon. And, rather than detract from the impact made by the soft red and creams of the toile de jouy against the varying greens of the washed walls, the curtains have been chosen to be in a soft, unobtrusive plain cream material. The cream matches the background colour of the toile, hence sharp contrast is avoided.

a certain blue-toned, chilly charm, is actually a very difficult colour to get right. Unfortunately, its then popularity meant that it – and its near neighbour, a yellow-toned pale green – were taken up, in the mid-twentieth century, by those who decreed the colours for school and hospital walls. Presumably it was thought that 'cool' and 'pale' were synonyms for 'calm' and 'reflection'. Too many public rooms and corridors, bathrooms and waiting rooms have been painted these cold blue-green shades as well as that particularly obnoxious shade of bilious yellow-green. Even more misguidedly, a gloss finish was often used to cover large areas, presumably because it was considered to be more durable. Durable it might have been, but it also was even colder than the same colour in a matt finish, reflecting the light in a particularly chilly fashion. In addition, whilst many light colours do not work particularly well in a gloss finish, cool, pale greens work least well of all. Dark glossy green,

THIS PAGE Apple green – Bramley apples, for preference – is a fresh and bright colour for a kitchen, so long as it is combined with other colours and textures that stop it becoming acid. In this New York kitchen and hallway, it has been teamed with the warm tones of pale wood, both on the floor and the doors of kitchen cabinets, and with an interesting pale blue-grey on the doors leading off the hallway, that is again taken up by the steel splash-back and kitchen table and chairs.

100 colours explored

on the other hand, can be very striking, and can be used in strong and effective contrast with any number of colours: mango and guava, powder pink, French mustard, pale lilac, for example, as well as white and buttermilk or cream.

Cool greens can be the clearest and most refreshing of shades, and greens used in conjunction with other greens can be extremely effective. That said, I think that the chilly coolness of very cool, light greens means that it is actually very difficult for these colours to work really effectively in a cool climate under a chilly natural light. Almost all cool, light greens need accent colours – pink, mango, terracotta, lemon or sunshine yellow. It is these that point out the depths of green and add a necessary reminder of warmth. Cool greens work better in some rooms than others – they are not colours for a bedroom, for example, as morning light and cool green do not make for the happiest of companions.

RIGHT A small shower room has been made into a room of bright green wit. The walls, even within the shower area, have been left rough-plastered and then coloured with a soft apple green – probably Granny Smith, this time. The fittings are stainless steel, and the sink has been dropped into a yellow-green Perspex surround; this almost neon material is also used for the shower screen.

BELOW, LEFT AND CENTRE Walls painted a bright, uncompromising fresh lime green are complemented by straight-backed chairs upholstered in a warm terracotta russet shade.
BELOW RIGHT To many, these sharp greens look artificial and unnatural. But you only need glance around you to see that they are the most natural colours of all: here, spring green at its most vivid – after the rain.

Yellows, oranges and golds

Yellow is a primary colour – a fact that has its advantages and disadvantages. Stronger than most other colours, it can dominate a scheme and make the colours around it seem dull and dirty. The other primaries – red and blue – are strong enough to stand up to a bright yellow scheme, yet the colours tend to sit uncomfortably together. At its most basic, orange – a most underestimated colour – is made from mixing red and yellow. That said, the tone of orange is very reliant on which yellow and which red are used, and how much of each. Bright reds and bright yellows make a brighter orange, whilst those colours mixed with white produce a warm peach. The bolder of these tones – along with gold – make wonderfully flattering accent colours, as well as being successful in their own right.

Yellows

YELLOW IS SAID TO BE TOO EMOTIONAL A COLOUR FOR SOME, BUT THE FACT IS THAT IT IS A STIMULATING COLOUR, AND CAN, WHEN USED PROPERLY, BRING A WARMTH, COLOUR AND WELCOME INTO COLD ROOMS LACKING IN SUNLIGHT. IT ALSO HAS THE PROPERTY OF ADVANCING INTO A ROOM AND SO CAN BE USED TO GIVE PROMINENCE TO OBJECTS, WHILST DISTRACTING THE EYE FROM OTHERS.

The variety of sources from which yellow dye has been laboriously made demonstrates the versatility of tone available. Yellows were extracted from pomegranate and lemon rinds, safflower petals and buds, and primroses. The very first yellows were made from the earth pigment ochre, a clay coloured by iron oxide, and the warm yellows we use today still have the same elemental feeling to them.

Yellow has long been revered in different cultures; it was the sacred colour of the Royal House in China, whose members were the only people allowed to wear yellow in their elaborate woven and embroidered silk costumes. Today it is used with more abandon, yet it still requires a certain confidence to get yellow right.

COOL YELLOW

Yellow is far more versatile than is often thought. As shown in medieval decoration, cool yellow harmonizes with white, purple, blue, violet and deep crimson. Many people are wary of yellow because, whilst a warm yellow – one with red in it – is exactly that (warm), a cool yellow can chill an atmosphere as soon as it is on

the wall. Think of the colour of lemons (in particular, the closeness between a lime and a lemon) or even of primroses. There is very little sunny warmth in either of these; their green tints make them interesting, even luminous, but they could never be considered warm. Canary yellow and daffodil yellow are also cool hues, and go with green-based tones as well as cool blues. In countries with a cool natural light, many yellows have a tendency to look greenish because of the slightly blue daylight, and they certainly reflect the outside light within their tones. Therefore, cool yellows, more than any other colour, should always be tested first on the walls before making a choice. They

ABOVE This palette of yellows is warmer and more subdued in tone than those used in the living room. Everything has been arranged to harmonize – the yellows have been combined with deeper, warmer shades from the same palette. The chair seat and even the tone of the floor fit into the same scheme. **BELOW, LEFT AND RIGHT** A bedroom in the same apartment has been outlined with the same technique as that of the living room. Panels have been suggested by using a deep orange wash over the yellow base coat, to suggest a frame around painted panels.

OPPOSITE In a Milanese living room, tones of yellow have been used particularly imaginatively. The clear yellow on the walls has been left in its pristine state, but each wall has been outlined by a wide all-round border of a deeper yellow wash that frames the wall. The addition of a fine white line separating the colours pulls the whole scheme together. The door frame is similarly coloured, whilst the door, unusually, has been stripped and bleached.

The walls of this nicely functional kitchen are painted a soft orange that veers towards brown and mustard tones. Against this background, the lower cabinets and a solitary wall-hung cupboard are painted a clear bright yellow. No clash, no competition, just harmony which never becomes dull. Every other element in the room is functional: the wooden work surface on one side of the cooker, the white worktop on the other. Interestingly, there is no colour in the choice of utensils and equipment — metal and whites — except for a single note of red, a colour from which the wall tone is derived.

RIGHT This kitchen clearly demonstrates how tones of a colour taken through a palette can be used to striking effect. The yellows and oranges of the walls and units perfectly complement the wooden furnishings, as well as the functional elements of the kitchen. **BELOW AND FAR RIGHT** These details – shiny chrome handles on a yellow background, a used wooden chopping board and an antique enamel jug – show how clever a background colour this subtle yellow is, and how suited it is to a functional role.

should really be used in sunny rooms but, that said, a classical Scandinavian combination is cool yellow with cool blue and a touch of white – supremely elegant, if rather chilly.

WARM YELLOWS

Of all its other connotations and associations, perhaps the most important by far is that yellow is the colour of the sun. One cannot help but want to be warmed by it and respond to its air of hope and clarity. One of the most striking uses of yellow ever, and now to be seen in its newly restored glory, is Sir John Soane's drawing room at his house in Lincoln's Inn Fields in London. First conceived in the eighteenth century, the walls are coloured in a brilliant, confident yellow, which gives everything in the room a meaning and a life without any feeling of domination. Other famous warm yellow rooms include the dining room in

Claude Monet's house at Giverny, in France, where the yellow walls work particularly well because of their close association with blue – perhaps one of the happiest of colour combinations.

Bright warm yellow is also interesting with dark warm colours such as chestnut or chocolate, and in particular with black. But softer warm yellows can also be very effective when they are used with equally soft contrasting shades.

Warm yellow also reflects other colours in the light source, so it is, again, important to try the shade you favour on a wall and see how it looks, as all yellows vary greatly as to character, intensity and hue. Although warm yellows are probably seen at their best in cold climes, where the light is cooler, yellows which are recognizably touched with warm light browns to create colours like straw and saffron can be very effective in strong light, like that of the Mediterranean.

BELOW In this living room, yellow beckons the visitor inwards. Appreciated for at least three hundred years as a colour against which to display paintings and objects, yellow is often best allowed to dominate a scheme, with every other element subordinate to it. Here, there is no other colour, only natural and neutral tones in the wooden furniture and floor, the black-and-white prints and the old leather armchair.

Yellow can be a demanding colour; a strong, Chinese lacquer yellow, for example, would simply be too much in many rooms. But it does depend greatly on the size of the room – a small room, like a bathroom or small kitchen, can look wonderful painted with lashings of flat, bright, sunny yellow, whilst a larger room, such as a bedroom or a living room, is happier when the yellow is toned down with a little cream. A yellow that has mixed into it a little brown and a little orange, as well as a dollop of cream, is

both welcoming and subtle. This is a colour with which to decorate and against which objects and ornaments stand out – the final effect is like ripe corn.

Warm yellow also looks good paired with wooden furniture – particularly the warmer shades like maple, walnut and waxed pine. It also makes a good background for black-painted or ebony pieces. A warm yellow that has more brown in it – more earth tones, in fact – looks its best when used with other earth tones and set against a polished wooden floor.

RIGHT Yellow is an interesting colour in that, although it can be very dominant, it is also a very welcoming colour, in whatever guise. Like the colour of a double-yolked, free-range egg, this rich yellow on the wall is warm and welcoming. Sensibly, there has been no attempt to match it or to fight against it. The woodwork is impressively white and the mantelpiece and fire surround have also been painted white – almost painted out. The only contrast – which is still in the same palette – comes from the portrait on the mantelpiece, in a limed-wood frame, and the covering of the rounded stool, as well as the naïve, brightly coloured mat in front of the fireplace.

Oranges

ORANGE IS A MIXTURE OF THE PRIMARY COLOURS RED AND YELLOW.
A BRIGHT RED AND A BRIGHT YELLOW, SUCH AS CADMIUM, GIVE THE
CLEAREST ORANGE; A BLUE-RED AND BLUE-YELLOW WILL GIVE A
QUIETER HUE, WHILE BROWN-REDS MAKE A MORE TERRACOTTA TONE.

Although, as explained above, mixing different tones of the two
primaries, yellow and red, will give softer or deeper oranges, it
is still the case that, because these two primaries are so strong
in themselves, in a decorative context orange must be employed with
care. This is probably why – although it has enjoyed short periods of
favour over the years – orange has not been more widely chosen as
an interior-decoration colour. But today, once again, the colour
orange is being appreciated for what it is – a life-enhancing colour
which can bring light and warmth into rooms and evoke feelings of
sunshine and fire and pleasure.

New subtle paint colours and paint techniques mean that the
orange seen today is very different from the dead, almost neon-like
colour we associate with the 1960s. Perhaps the key to using
orange successfully lies first with the word itself. Unlike the names
of other colours – red, for example, where one person might see
deep cherry whilst another sees hot pillar-box – to most people, the
word 'orange' immediately summons up the bright, glowing strong
colour of the eponymous citrus fruit. So perhaps, instead of thinking

OPPOSITE BOTTOM Perhaps one of the most obvious – and certainly one of the most successful – colour combinations is orange and blue. As a couple, these two will rarely misfire. That said, the ratios of each must be considered with care, as they can easily overpower. In this cheering shower room, encouragement to get up and go in the morning is given with the bright orange tiles, emphasized by the soft blue of the tiles surrounding the shower as well as the blue door.

MAIN, ABOVE AND BELOW In a relaxed and friendly room, tones of yellow and cream predominate, complemented by pale, polished wooden floors and furnishings and white walls. The calm colours are brought into relief by the single slash of colour – an orange sliding partition that separates the bedroom from the living room. This room is a good example of orange used as an accent colour: any more would simply be too much; any less, and the room could well slide into the mundane.

about how to use orange in a room, it would be easier to think first of other words that conjure up some of the many tones and shades that are also part of the vibrancy of pure orange. One could imagine, for example, the rich orange-brown tones of African earth; the almost-brown, textured feel of chunky dark marmalade; flickering, fugitive tongues of a flame; the milky tones of orange butter icing, or the watery tones of diluted squash. There are hues of orange, too, in other fruits and flowers, like ripe apricots and golden-orange plums and, richest of all, the juicy deep tones of blood-orange flesh; think of fragile Iceland poppies, the delicate petals of Oriental poppies, and the autumnal fiery and russet tones of late summer dahlias.

With these images in mind, suddenly the range and scope of orange becomes apparent, and the numerous ways in which it might be used in the home can be explored to the full. And, once an idea of a

In earthy tones or tangerine bright, orange is the colour of life – of light and warmth, of sun-filled days and roaring fires.

subtle tone or shade takes hold, the sophisticated paint techniques available today mean that the colour can be applied, perhaps as a soft watery glaze or even in deep, rich enamel-like layers.

But, however much you adore these new oranges, it is still important to choose carefully where to use them best in the home. Orange is far more suitable for some rooms than others; many people, for instance, would probably not care to have orange in a bedroom, however light in tone and whatever the shade. In the wrong light, it could either appear bilious and cold, or else far too strong and unforgiving. But orange in the dining room or kitchen, now that would be a different matter altogether. With its rich warm tones, orange would benefit the coldest kitchen and would make an already-warm room appear positively womb-like. It works so well, too, with many contemporary kitchen combinations, particularly those ubiquitous cooking and working surfaces, such as stainless steel, shiny

OPPOSITE MAIN There are no halfway measures here. This kitchen has been painted in an unequivocal orange. Although the traditional flagstoned floors, old wooden tables and countertops and enamel weighing machine and pots and jugs all look very much at home, so equally do the professional range and grill — more homely here than industrial — fitted into the original stone fireplace.

OPPOSITE INSETS A kitchen as warm as this would simply not look right with all its tools hidden away behind doors. Hung, propped or stacked against the walls, their shapes and tones contrast with the deep-toned wall behind.

ABOVE This clever colour works just as well in a contemporary setting as it does in a more traditional and rural environment. Here the deep burnt orange background throws the kitchen

furnishings and appliances into sharp relief. The brushed-steel hood and shiny stainless-steel tools above the burners combine with the pale wooden cabinets and rough slate surround and countertop to give a clear contrast to the tones of walls.

RIGHT Even the simple kitchen taps here look striking against this strong contrast of textures and colours. Is there no end to orange's versatility?

ABOVE AND LEFT Although it might seem a contradiction in terms, warm orange used in a sunny climate can work very well. The trick is that it must have enough brown in it. When successful, far from overheating the room, a burnt orange like this gives a feeling of the coolness of earth, an almost vegetal sense of pigment and colour. The sensation would have been lost, however, if the surrounding colours were also in such strong shades; instead, neutrals – creams, whites and biscuit – are the accompanying hues.

metal, rough slate and bleached wood – they all appear in wonderfully sharp and edgy modern contrast to orange's rounded tones.

Orange dining rooms may, at first thought, seem to be a bit much, but actually, in its deeper, darker incarnation, orange can be about as good a dining colour as you can hope to get. Consider the traditional reds used in eating rooms – they tended to contain a lot of brown, bringing them closer to terracotta. And a similar brown-orange will look as successful today. Many people like to eat by candlelight in the evenings, and deep-orange walls will make the most of the candles' glow.

In a living room, too, although it might not be the colour that is first thought of, orange can be just the thing to lighten and warm a coolly lit room, and will make a sunny room positively Mediterranean.

Surprisingly, remembering the decorative faux pas of the 1960s, orange is a very forgiving colour: it can look deeply traditional, as well as boldly contemporary. The browns and reds of antique furniture, wood and

Oranges that are melted down and whipped up with paler tones become the most useful and adaptable of colours.

ABOVE AND LEFT In some situations, deep orange can be considered an over-stimulating colour – too vigorous, almost. However, it can also be a colour which encourages concentration and production. It is peaceful and calm, without being soporific and, in the same way that deep orange is successful in the kitchen, it can give a sense of purpose to a workroom. In this home office, for example, there are no disturbing contrasts – all the elements are chosen to work together in harmony. The palette is very much a combination of earth and autumn colours and textures, with polished wood, dark-brown leather and a neutral, natural floor covering that all harmonize perfectly with the walls. The overall effect is one of industry rather than stress.

yellows, oranges and golds **115**

THIS PAGE This Paris bedroom is the colour of a basket of ripe apricots. On the walls is matt peach paint; behind the bed is an elaborate, embroidered headboard in pale tones of peach, green and warm cream. The heavy luxury of a silk bed-cover in a colour like a ripe melon adds even more richness to a sybaritic scene. Although difficult to get right, these soft tones of pink-orange can be very effective when mixed with care. There should be no apology for unabashed femininity, and they work best with accents of slightly deeper pink-orange tones, like those of the pleated silk lampshade here.

brick complement it well, due to its affinity to the red-earth colour used in traditional decorating, from ancient Pompeii to contemporary Tuscany. Orange has within it many of the tones of warm wood – from pine to mahogany – and, as such, is a colour that can look very fitting in a room with panelling or a lot of wood furniture, or in a room where a wooden floor is dominant. Simply add an accent of bright red, perhaps in cushions or a rug. Orange also has the ability to warm a room that is panelled in overly dark wood. And, surprisingly, this colour can cool – with the addition of some white – a room that is overly yellow in feeling, one furnished with stripped pine and floored with pine boards, perhaps.

Orange, like its stronger sister red, also works well as an accent colour, pointing out the merits of other colours within a scheme, such as various purples and mauves, as well as darkest green, grey-olive green and warm flannel grey. Ideas for working with orange in this way – like so many other colour ideas for the home – can be lifted from the garden, where orange is used by garden designers to add sophisticated accents in the border. Think of a late summer border: warm oranges, moving towards red and russet in hue, with touches of dark green, aubergine and purple. Again like red, orange is used in the garden to lift other colour schemes – particularly palettes of blue, and even some pinks; and oranges and russets mix well with purple-leaved shrubs, as well as with silver- or grey-leaved plants.

Learn from the ways in which nature uses oranges, from earthy brown tones to fiery hues, the soft apricots to the tangerine brights. The decorating world is, it could be said, your orange!

THIS PAGE Orange is again used in a bedroom, but this time in strong masculine contrast to the femininity illustrated opposite. Almost neoclassical in style and context, this room has deep flame-coloured walls, which make a vibrant background for the groups of pictures set in bold, gold frames. Many of these pictures are mounted on card of flannel grey and, in a subtle colour-considerate touch, the fringed, silk lampshade in front is also in grey. There is deeper contrast, too, in the dark-blue self-patterned bed-cover and curtains, and the deep aubergine headboard with a Greek key design. An orange colour scheme nearly always benefits from a shot of green – which can, and should, vary from cool to warm green, depending on which shade of orange is dominant. The upholstery on the chair provides the perfect accent.

THIS PAGE The gold element in this tiny dressing room is subtle, achieved more through textile and texture rather than pure colour. A canopied bed – very far from the traditional, heavy-weight four-poster – is hung with a delicately embroidered material with gold and brown stitching on a cream background. On the underside of the canopy is a second textile, embroidered with elegant beasts. The bed is simply furnished with a bolster and bed-cover in heavy cream, with a central strip of fabric that tones with the side curtains, but which brings a deeper tone to the white-gold of the curtain.

Golds

NOT ONLY HAS GOLD BEEN A COLOUR OF ROMANTIC AND HISTORICAL
SIGNIFICANCE IN ITS OWN RIGHT, IT HAS ALSO ALWAYS PLAYED AN
IMPORTANT PART, IN DECORATIVE TERMS, IN ALLEVIATING THE STRENGTH
AND BRIGHTNESS OF OTHER COLOURS.

From medieval times to the present day, gold has been used to break
up blocks of other colour as well as outlining and underlining colour
combinations. Gold – even a fine line – gives a richness and depth
to a scheme that cannot be achieved with other colours alone. An
edging, a soft touch, highlights and gives an air of more or less
subdued splendour in a room. Of course, gold can also be used
resplendent in its solitary glory – fantastic in a reception room or
a dining room, where candlelight flickers against the burnished
surface. In the eighteenth century, they understood the romantic,
almost magical atmosphere engendered by gold. What often seems
to us too much, when we look at carved and gilded furniture from
the past, should be imagined as it was more usually seen then, lit
by candlelight, with every surface twinkling and shimmering, caught
in the wavering light. Use it thus today, in areas and arrangements
where its magical subtlety can be appreciated and seen at its best.

THIS PAGE Even when gold is used
subtly, it has an air of the exotic,
and when it is displayed in all its
glory – as it is here – it is
breathtaking. In this Manhattan
apartment, walls have been
completely covered in gold leaf,
which has immense depth of tone
and a gleaming lustre. Against this
exotic background, artefacts and
furniture of some strength are
needed – and are supplied with
a tribal carving on one wall and
a simple, dramatic African bench
with a jute-covered cushion on the
other. There is not even the
intrusion of a door frame; the door
is practically invisible except for
a brightly beaded key tassel – in
keeping with the ethnic theme.

Colours in
combination

The best combinations of colour – in no matter what colour spectrum – have an element of surprise. This idea of a surprise is an important one. On entering a room you should think: how nice, how interesting – and how unusual!

In one sense, all colours should only be used in combination, for a single colour on its own is meaningless, only acquiring meaning when it is juxtaposed to another colour, however subtle the contrast. Our eye and brain respond to colour *relationships* rather than to absolute colour.

Most people know well enough what, in their wardrobe, goes with what. They know through trial and error that a certain sweater works better with one skirt than another, and which shoes work with which outfit. And the reason they know is because they devote some time to thinking about it – and they look carefully and truthfully. That is what you have to do when combining colours in interior decoration, too.

To continue with the wardrobe analogy: in the same way that just a touch of red, say in the shoes, might work with an otherwise green ensemble, when combining colours in a room, it is important to think about in what proportions two or more colours should be combined. When you are going to combine colours on the walls, you probably try them on a piece of card to see how they look together. But remember that the relative size of the surfaces to be coloured should also be taken into account – two chosen colours may look fine as small dabs, but if one is used over an entire wall and the other is merely covering the skirting board, the relationship may not work. Remember, too, that the changing light source also affects the tone of the colour, which in turn affects what we see.

The most important thing, as with every aspect of interior decoration, is to think bold and to think broad – which is not, by the way, the same as harsh or strident.

OPPOSITE Milky-brown walls mixed with a little purple – a colour sometimes called taupe – are gentle and welcoming. Hung against this warm background, above the wooden bench, are three perfectly placed paintings of subtly changing colour by the owner, artist Andrew Wallace. The final effect is an essay in soft-toned harmony.
PREVIOUS PAGE This apartment exhibits a brave contrast of bright colour that works wonderfully. The tangerine and electric blue have been diffused with a wall of glass bricks and a translucent corrugated plastic screen, which serve to dilute any stridency the combination might have had.

A lesson in tone

THERE IS REALLY NO SUCH THING AS AN UNUSUAL COLOUR SCHEME. EVERY COLOUR SCHEME IS UNUSUAL IN THAT EACH IS INDIVIDUAL — A LIST OF THE COLOURS USED SAYS NOTHING ABOUT THE SUBTLETIES OF A PARTICULAR COMBINATION. SUCCESSFUL SCHEMES WORK BECAUSE THE COLOUR IS CLEVERLY USED RATHER THAN CLEVERLY CHOSEN.

ABOVE AND BELOW In the bedroom, irregular, horizontal bands of colour are pulled together by the colour used on the tall windows, the floor-to-ceiling surrounds of which have been painted in a pale grey-green, as have the panelled internal shutters and the woodwork beneath the windows. The colour is not cold — a small amount of yellow has been added, which acts as a link between the woodwork and the yellow-toned colours of the walls. When several different colours are being used together in one room, it is very important to take into account what colour the different areas of woodwork are to be. They do not all have to be the same.

There are some who understand better than others how to use colour, and Lindsay Taylor's apartment represents a comprehensive course in lateral — as well as vertical — colour thinking, in addition to providing a knowledgeable lesson in colour combining. Her palette includes grey-blue, lilac, mint green, sun-faded terracotta, pale yellow and ochre, and is used to fascinating effect.

The apartment is not a modern one and therefore benefits from high ceilings, large windows and self-assured wooden surrounds to the windows and doors, as well as bold plaster ceiling cornices — all the sort of architectural detail that was common in the nineteenth century, but which is rarely found today in more modern spaces. These structural elements give an extra depth to her painting schemes, transforming the walls from flat canvases, as it were, into three-dimensional works.

It is not just that every room is painted in different imaginative and subtle colour combinations, but even more interesting is the wit and imagination she has employed in the way that she has arranged the colour on the walls. In the kitchen, for example, there are wide vertical panels of colour — lilac, butternut squash, purple —

sometimes with a panel divided from the next by a straight edge, sometimes by an edge of waves.

In the bedroom, a more muted scheme uses wide — very wide — horizontal panels of colour. From ground level, an ochre panel which is mantelpiece height; then a central band of pale grey which rises to envelop the picture rail; and, between that and the cornice, a band of terracotta pink. Other woodwork is painted grey-green. Although complex, this palette, based on earth-toned colours, works together in a wonderfully soothing combination, conducive to sleep.

THIS PAGE In the bedroom, the broad stripes of colour on the walls are part of an earth-toned palette based on yellows and browns: ochre covers the lowest section; grey (albeit a grey of a soft creamy tone) is the central slice; and the upper section to the ceiling is a pale terracotta. The floor is made of chipboard sections and has been left in its natural state.

LEFT In the living room, a section of wall painted dusky pink meets a section painted in a soft red. The colour of the upholstery of the sofa echoes the wall behind.

In the sitting room, aquamarine marches across one wall to the fireplace. The colours throughout the room are inspired by the earthy rich tones of India and Indian miniatures, so dusty pinks, soft reds and saffron yellow are all included in the mix. At the fireplace the colour changes to yellow. Yellow takes up the baton across the remainder of the wall, turning the corner onto the window wall where, two-thirds of the way across the window, yellow suddenly stops and a dusky pink takes over, sliding round the next corner to be met halfway across by a deeper soft red. The ceiling, its cornice and the upper section of the wall are all coloured in the same pale lilac, and the sofa, which sits in front of the double pink wall, is covered in fabrics that exactly match the background. Grounding this quiet explosion of colour is a carpet in a neutral grey – the 'mouseback' shade endorsed

The contrasts do not – as you might expect – give a feeling of jumpy energy; rather they engender a sense of extreme relaxation, like a sunny June day.

ABOVE Once again, colour lessons can be found in the natural world. The range of colours that have their base in yellow tones is, in nature, wide and rich, and can encourage us to combine these boldly.
RIGHT In the kitchen–dining room the walls have been painted with vertical bands of colour, some of which look as if they have been attacked by a giant pair of pinking shears. The wavy edge was in fact hand-painted by the owner. The success of the lilac and yellow combination is due to the fact that both colours are of the same strength. Because these colours are so bright, the woodwork has been painted in a neutral cream.

by designer John Fowler, perhaps? The overall effect
is soothing rather than jarring.

Another subtlety, that is not immediately apparent
in the clever colour ways of this apartment, is the fact
that, although colour is presented in the same way
throughout the space – using wide connecting bands
of different shades – each room is slightly different in
its application. In the bedroom, the colour is divided
vertically, in the sitting room horizontally, and in the
kitchen with humorous handpainted touches.

Lindsay Taylor's glorious apartment is one that
should be studied carefully by all amateurs – and,
indeed, experts – of colour and interior decoration.
Seemingly so simple and understated as to be almost
naïve, there are in fact enough clever and dynamic
touches and ideas here to inspire even the most
sophisticated of decorative artists.

LEFT The sunny aspect of this
room is emphasized by the pink and
yellow window wall. The handsome
windows, as well as the shutters,
are painted in three different
colours, matching the horizontal
stripes and vertical bands and
blending into the total scheme.

BELOW A vertically striped wall –
part aquamarine, part an orange-
toned yellow – meet above the
fireplace, but not at the obvious
halfway mark. A single, well-
chosen bowl and the marble of
the fire surround emphasize the
colour combination.

RIGHT Nothing in this corner has been left to chance and all the features combine to produce a completely harmonious group. Not only are the colours of the chair soft, Irish and heather-toned, but also the checks on the tweed act as definition. The lichen grey-green of the wooden panelling is exactly right as a background. Nothing jars or is ill-at-ease – even the coloured glasses on the side table pick up the moorland mood.

BELOW The truth of this colour scheme is verified by seeing the real thing. In this attention to detail lies the success of the decorative plan. Texture and pattern are as important as the colours themselves in creating a harmonious – and believable – colour palette taken from nature. Outside, rough is paired with smooth, soft with hard; texture is all-important, and it is essential to add that element to an interior colour scheme.

Gaelic blend

NATURE ALMOST ALWAYS GETS IT RIGHT – THAT IS WHERE COLOUR DESIGN STARTED, AFTER ALL. IN THIS PARISIAN APARTMENT THE COLOURS OF AN IRISH MOOR ARE TRANSFERRED TO THE CITY WITH CHARM AND SUBTLETY.

To copy nature's colour combinations is not to be undertaken in a slapdash manner; instead it requires application and study. 'Subtlety' is the key word here – just throwing different shades together and hoping they will look like a wild-flower meadow or a misty-toned moorland will rarely work. But in this apartment it works brilliantly, because its designer-owner has transferred the memories of her Irish heritage to a range of furniture and textiles and then combined them with Celtic inspiration. Lilacs, mauves, clover pinks, moss greens, lichen greys and heather honeys are the textile colours; linens and tweeds, plaids and voiles are the textiles themselves; and all work together in the centre of Paris just as they do on the moors. And, although the fabrics and colours work well on their own, what really pulls the look together are the soft, beguiling paint tones on the walls, all different, but still remaining within the moorland palette. The effect is overwhelmingly evocative.

ABOVE LEFT, CENTRE AND RIGHT
As you enter this tall-windowed sitting room, you are immediately transported far away to the traffic-free uplands. The whole picture shows that it is important to lavish colour and to use a broad-based palette. If the colours used here had been limited to two or three of the heather tones, the room would have lacked depth and interest. But by using at least half a dozen colours on furniture, curtains and walls, the eye remains interested and involved, and the desired harmony is achieved. If all the tones are taken from one palette, even if they are used in deeper strengths, then they can all be mixed with abandon and added to at will.

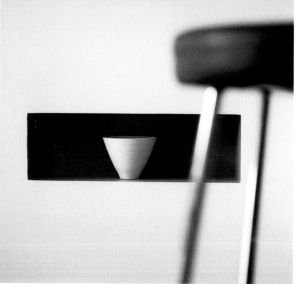

ABOVE AND ABOVE LEFT Against a white wall, a series of seemingly randomly placed niches have been cut into the plaster and painted in different and contrasting tones, from soft white to deep chocolate. In each space a small simple object is displayed. It is a simple but ingenious idea that both breaks up a large area of wall, as well as becoming a focal point of real decorative interest.

LEFT In the foreground, in front of the white wall, a slate-topped dining table is partnered by chairs that have been upholstered in lilac. The colours sit comfortably together without sharp contrast. The wall that leads away from the dining area is a deep mushroom brown.

Nearly neutrals

ALTHOUGH PERHAPS THE MOST ESSENTIAL CHARACTERISTIC OF A NO-COLOUR OR NEUTRAL SCHEME IS THAT THE FINAL LOOK SHOULD BE WARM AND RICH AND TEXTURAL, THESE RATHER NEBULOUS QUALITIES ARE PROBABLY THE MOST DIFFICULT TO ACHIEVE. THE DESIRED EFFECT MUST BE INTERNATIONAL JET SET, NOT INSTITUTIONAL WET SET.

LEFT Texture is used to avoid any suggestion of monotony: an armchair is upholstered in heavy white, dressed with a soft, grey mohair throw, to which is added the luxury of a striped, fur cushion. **BELOW** A seating area, with large cushions in differing tones of brown, is arranged beneath a series of wall panels which range from milk chocolate brown to taupe, and pale aubergine to palest lilac.

No-colour colours – boringly known as neutrals, a term which gives no hint of their richness and diversity – are those colours that are most associated with the natural world, like stone, sand and pebbles, wheat, biscuit, mushrooms and ivory, mole and mouse. They generally stem from brown or grey and the variations are infinite.

As a rule, greys are cool neutrals and browns warm neutrals, the luminosity of the former being higher than that of the latter. A pearly grey compounded with a brilliant white is far more lively and luminous than a brown in which there is not enough yellow.

Neutrals are much affected by the light around them, so each must be considered in its own right. Texture is also important when no-colour colours are used – matt surfaces should be paired with shiny, rough with smooth, soft with hard. These differences are important because a room decorated in neutral tones should glow and shine, each surface both complimenting as well as complementing the others.

However, texture alone is not enough. Even the warmest neutral scheme really needs a dash of colour in its life: something sharp, bright and strong that will bring the scheme to life; for unrelenting neutral tones do run the risk of arriving at insipidity rather than the desired elan.

The apartment seen here is not large – in fact it is small and the choice of neutrals is the right one, as they expand the space in a subtle way. Although they may be allowed to predominate in a scheme, neutrals should not be all-prevailing. The neutral colour palette here includes soft grey, grey-lilac and mushroom with, where appropriate, some deeper shades within the same palette, like aubergine,

chocolate brown and slate. These darker, stronger shades emphasize the appealing pallor of the lighter neutrals. Note that the stronger colours are not contrasting; they are all darker shades of their paler cousins, which is why the overall effect is so happy.

There should always be a touch of colour somewhere within a neutral palette.

The planes of soft colour are used to extend the eye and to suggest volume and area where none exist. They work also to direct the eye elsewhere – around a corner perhaps, towards a new point of interest. Incidentally, decorative clutter is also kept to a minimum, and a clever and practical idea, which keeps flat surfaces free as

well as adding decorative interest, is the display alcoves of different sizes cut into one wall. Painting some alcoves in contrasting, dark colours, all within a brown palette, makes a further strong decorative statement.

In the living room, floorboards are painted in a dark, gloss brown, which, with its hint of purple, looks warm rather than institutional. Painted floorboards are a useful way of bringing colour into a room, but the choice of colour itself should be carefully considered. Stay away from any colour or finish which smacks of backstairs or institutional living.

Once again, texture is cleverly used: a screen in the bedroom, rather than being painted, has been upholstered in grey velvet. A table top is made of slate instead of wood; a pale armchair has a mohair throw in grey as well as a warm fur cushion. All these touches add warmth and personality to this sophisticated colour blend.

THIS PAGE The sleeping area is surprising and pleasing in its conjunction of comfort with rigorous colour principles. At the foot of the bed and against pale lilac walls and cream woodwork is a grey velvet upholstered board which conceals a clothes-hanging rail. A dark antique bed on an oak parquet floor contrasts with the walls. Sheer curtains of a grey-silver weave diffuse the natural light.

THIS PAGE Although this is a
textbook combination of muted
neutral colour, the different
elements in the central area are
literally grounded by the floor. The
walls are coloured in a soft snow-
cloud beige, and the fireplace and
mantelpiece are a pale mushroom
shade. The chairs and the stool fit
well into the muted theme and even
the artwork is within the same
palette. But none of it would work
so well were it not for the wooden
floorboards, which have been
painted an unusual and dramatic
dark brown, which has more than a
hint of purple in it – like a
Mediterranean aubergine.

Harmonious hues

A LARGE SPACE, BLESSED WITH NATURAL LIGHT, CAN TAKE A MORE DRAMATIC AND CONFIDENT USE OF COLOUR THAN A SMALL ONE. AN EFFECTIVE TREATMENT IN SUCH A ROOM IS TO COMBINE MANY HUES, EACH WITHIN THE SAME COLOUR RANGE AND OF SIMILAR STRENGTH AND TONE, YET EACH SLIGHTLY DIFFERENT FROM THE NEXT.

Although, in theory, any range of any colour could be used in a generously proportioned, well-lit room, the fact is that care must be taken not to choose a tone that is too much of anything – too bright, too dark, too strong or too light. Dark shades, for example, have the effect of seeming to make walls recede, so in a large room too dark a tone would make the room seem as if it were the interior of an endless cavern; equally, too vivid a colour – bright purple or the brightest of oranges – would be too strong, without respite and too difficult to live with. It is, as always, a question of appropriateness.

OPPOSITE Pink, unlike red, is a feminine colour; it gives a feeling of light, warmth and welcome, but it requires confidence to allow pink to predominate in a room. Harmony is essential: of colour, of line and of texture. Here the tone is just right. This room is not painted in solid, flat colour. Everywhere there are variations on a coloured and textured theme. On the living-room walls, for example, panelling is used to make a point: within the panel there is one tone of pink, the panel moulding is itself a brighter pink, and the wall on the other side of the moulding is a softer coral-tinted pink, which has been dragged. The curtains also add a textural contrast, made as they are in unlined pink silk, which filters and diffuses the light.

When combining hues from the same section of the colour wheel, success comes if the majority of the colours are of the same strength – that is, if each one has the same amount of white in it, since the eye accepts with ease colours that have the same amount of tonality. This not only works when you are trying to use different colours in one range; it also works when you are using colours which are in contrast to each other – like yellow and blue, for example. As long as they are the same strength – that is to say, neither one is much deeper nor much paler than the other, and both are warm or cold – they will tend to work together.

That said, schemes using hues of one colour family rarely work well unless there is one shade within that scheme that is deeper and stronger than the others, even though it is in the same colour range. It is as if that one slightly discordant note ties everything together. Often it need only be a single line of colour: a painted dado rail – real or trompe l'oeil – or a raised moulding on a shutter or door panel; no matter how seemingly insignificant, it has an influence beyond its presence. This effect is demonstrated in this Paris apartment, where shades from pink through coral to orange are brought to heel by the clever use of gilding.

THIS PAGE In the dining room of designer Geraldine Prieur's Paris apartment, the walls are washed in dusky pink with overlaid washed stripes of pale melon. The bureau is painted soft peach, and the ornate gold chandelier above has soft pink shades. On the bureau is a selection from the range of ceramics and glassware designed by Geraldine Prieur, combining gold and berry pink – a theme echoed throughout the apartment. It has all been done with a lightness of touch which is essential when one colour is dominant.

Complementary clash

COMPLEMENTARY COLOURS ARE ALWAYS INTERESTING WHEN USED TOGETHER, ALTHOUGH IT IS IMPORTANT TO GET THE PROPORTIONS RIGHT, WITH NOT TOO MUCH OR TOO LITTLE OF EACH. HERE, ORANGE AND BLUE ARE CUT WITH A TELLING DASH OF PINK.

In the days when clean white cotton gloves were de rigueur and hats were worn with the shoes that matched the handbag, there was a rather cruel fashion dictum on colour which extolled the combination of pink and navy as being 'the plain girl's last hope' – meaning, one presumes, that the combination was always, and in any circumstance, a flattering one.

As in fashion, so in life, and in this open-plan city apartment, pink and deep blue – the navy of today – as well as orange, are used in combination with other structural and visual elements to define and shape the space.

Although at first sight the liberal use of colour seems almost indiscriminate, there are clearly defined colour stories throughout the apartment. First is the relationship between blue and orange, which, as they are complementary colours on the colour wheel, will always work together and emphasize each other – although to achieve success it is important to use such definite colours in equal strengths, as has been done here. Next, and just as important, is the use of soft pink – first, as we mentioned above, in its role as a harmonious partner for deep blue and, second, playing its part in a subtle, familial combination with orange. This shade of pink is also

ABOVE Orange and blue are contrasted but also diluted by the plywood work surface, as well as by the multicoloured mosaic tiles.
RIGHT The kitchen area of this apartment is designed with curves and colour; an undulating work surface of polished plywood has bright orange cupboards beneath and angular orange open shelves above. Behind the worktop is a panel of mosaic in assorted blues, and above that is a wall in blue – the signature colour of the apartment.

LEFT In the eating area, the clover-pink wall in the kitchen is echoed in the surface of the table, which links the two areas. The wall of clear glass bricks that runs beside the table is studded – seemingly at random – with bricks of blue glass. This wall plays an important part in the overall design of the apartment, as it diffuses the bright colours and gives them a necessary subtlety.

ABOVE This overview of the living area of the apartment and the kitchen beyond shows the way the colours are combined and contrasted. When colours as dominant as these are used in such close combination, it is important that other details and elements are refined to an almost spartan simplicity. The curved partition wall is unadorned and the floor is almost industrial in appearance.

used in its pale entirety in the soothing bedroom, where it is simply combined with white.

Perhaps more important than either the orange or the pink is the blue: bright but deep, welcoming but sophisticated, it is used as an architectural tool to give solidity to a curved wall, as decorative punctuation on chairs and accessories, and as a unifying element set as random insets in the otherwise clear glass wall, as well as in the mosaic tiles that figure in both the kitchen and bathroom. The clarity and strength of the ubiquitous blue is both emphasized and

The painted curves, the architectural curves, and even the curves of the moulded chairs, add fluidity to the whole painterly effect.

OPPOSITE The far side of the living area with a view into the bathroom beyond, partly hidden by a sliding door. Again, all the colours, although so bright and strong, work together as a composition. The bathroom, in an echo of the wall of glass bricks, has a wall of opaque corrugated plastic which is mirrored in the panels surrounding the bath.
LEFT A detail of the curved design and the contrasting blues of the apartment's dividing wall which masks the kitchen.

complemented by the rubber floor, which is powder blue with a quiet sheen – soft enough to work with the very pale pink of the bedroom, modern enough to act as a foil for the strongest of blues, and subtle enough to place the orange firmly in its place.

Comparing or referring a designer's architectural use of colour with the work of the late Mexican architect Luis Barragán is almost now a design cliché, but in truth Barragán's use of clear bright colour as an architectural tool is, in this apartment, acknowledged. A sliding door is painted bright orange, a curved wall in strong blues. Like some giant contemporary canvas, the colours constantly carry the eye from one area to another. It is worth pointing out that although the colours here have been used with such exuberance and, indeed, flamboyance, great discipline has been shown in any extra decoration. All accessories are limited to a strict palette of blue, white and chrome, and it is this attention to detail that ensures the success of such a strong scheme.

The way that light has been employed in this apartment is also very important. Throughout the space, the natural light is diffused – first with a wall of glass bricks, and second with an internal wall of clear, corrugated plastic that is between the bathroom and bedroom. Light is softened and reflected. Every colour benefits, taking on a warm soft hue that would not necessarily be apparent in the cool northern light.

LEFT A further view into the bathroom shows that the wall opposite the plastic screening is also covered with mosaic tiling – appropriate and practical for a bathroom, but also serving as a visual link with the other parts of the apartment; particularly the kitchen, which has the same tiling for the splash-back and the glass wall inset with blue bricks. Although the use of strong colour throughout this apartment is daring, it is also extremely disciplined – no other colours are allowed to intrude into the scheme, nor are there any irrelevant details of any description.

ABOVE It takes a bold eye and hand to use red on red like this, broken only by the glimmer of the chrome, the depth of the black and the brilliance of the white. Once again, strong colour must be arranged and selected with the utmost discipline, without any outside distraction. It must be said that, for many, this is not an easy scheme either to emulate or to live with.

RIGHT The coffee table is made from three simple pieces of clear glass so that it does not offer any distraction from the dominant colour theme, and its only decoration are three bowls – in black and red, naturally.

Twentieth-century tone

ALTHOUGH IT IS NOT EASY TO DO SUCCESSFULLY, WHEN IT IS EXECUTED WITH AS MUCH PANACHE AS HAS BEEN DONE IN THIS LIGHT-FILLED MANHATTAN APARTMENT, RED AND BLACK AND WHITE, FILLETED WITH SLIVERS OF SILVER, IS POSSIBLY ONE OF THE MOST EXCITING COLOUR COMBINATIONS IN CONTEMPORARY INTERIOR DECORATION.

ABOVE LEFT Contrast of texture is an important – indeed, a vital – theme in this dramatic apartment. The raised motifs on the thick, red rug not only contrast with the cool, glossy furniture and floor surface, they also add a vital warmth to what could otherwise be a rather chilly atmosphere.

ABOVE RIGHT The cool shiny surfaces are an admirable foil for the sculptural lines of the pieces of twentieth-century furnishing classics – as well as for the elegantly beribboned dog!

The three primary colours are, as every good schoolchild knows, red, yellow and blue; by definition, they are pure colours – the brightest – and when mixed together in pairs they can produce three other colours: the secondary ones of purple, orange and green. In principle, the three primaries, with the addition of the all-important black and white, can make up every colour that there is. This educational preamble serves to emphasize the point that these pure colours, because of their intensity, should be used with relative caution and skill in interior decoration.

Of all the primaries, it is red that is the most challenging. Red has an intensity that can swing from welcome to war in a moment. It is an exciting colour – for some, perhaps too exciting. When you use red decoratively, it can either be diluted and pared down or used at full strength, although there are not many who have the confidence to use red in this manner. However, John Barman, American interior designer and owner of this Manhattan apartment, is one who has no such qualms.

The living and dining area in Barman's apartment is enormous – measuring 10 x 8 metres (32 x 26 feet) – and is surrounded by huge windows which flood the space in natural light. An area as large as this, and filled with windows, is in fact one of the few decorative situations where bright and strong colours can be used together with impunity. Red, black and white, which would be overpowering together in a space of more modest dimensions, are uplifting and energizing here. The sharp splashes of brightest red

White is offset by touches of black and positively vibrates with the red, giving an instant feeling of pleasure.

come mostly from the iconic pieces of twentieth-century furniture that John Barman collects. Eames, Saarinen, Mies van der Rohe – examples of their work are to be found throughout the apartment, where they thrive through being displayed in so simple a style.

In medieval decoration – those brilliant flights of contained fancy that covered the walls and ceilings of Gothic buildings – bright colours such as red were either painted on, or separated from, other colours by areas of black or white. John Barman has taken this principle and used it to great contemporary effect in this high-flown setting. For him, white is not a neutral shade but a colour in its own right; although it is so often mistakenly used as a safe no-colour colour, white is actually far harder to live up to than a more forgiving off-white such as cream, ivory, bone or stone. Pure white looks best as part of a very positive colour plan; it needs a setting of drama and style, so if you're frightened of colour don't think about using it.

The other important aspect of this apartment is the way that texture has been employed: the strength of the various reds is made more acceptable to the eye by the fact that they are all in different finishes. Leather, cloth, glass and woven wool all add a depth and interest to the scheme that would not be there were the colour presented at one simple level.

More texture of a different nature is provided by the surface of the multi-dimensional 1970s screen with its slightly disquieting design of mirrored hemispheres, and the floor made from poured concrete which has been polished. As they quietly shine, both these elements – coupled with glimmers of chrome and stainless steel – all add a light-reflective quality to the entire scheme.

This Manhattan apartment is a hymn in praise of the pleasures of seemingly obvious, but none the less dramatic and striking, twentieth-century colour combinations. These are emphasized by classic pieces of furniture which could stand alone as sculptural pieces.

OPPOSITE TOP The spectators of this dramatic Park Avenue vista can enjoy the experience seated on chrome-and-red chairs around a 1950s white circular table by Eero Saarinen. Even the urban landscape seems specially designed to complement the scheme. No other decorative accessories are necessary.

OPPOSITE BELOW The silver-coated screen with its mirrored hemispheres provides more than enough decoration and colour for this area of the apartment. Dark-grey upholstered chairs sit in quiet contrast.

BELOW It is interesting that, although everything in this room exudes self-confidence, each element works well together with the next: the red wool rug from the 1970s complements the red leather chairs designed by Mies van der Rohe in 1929, whilst the black sofa and the smoked-glass coffee table cool the hot colour combinations. Accessories are also in period – mid-twentieth-century collectors' pieces of glass and ceramic which confirm the room's iconic status.

Autumn light

ALTHOUGH CLEVER COLOUR COMBINATIONS CAN BE ACHIEVED BY USING CONTRASTING COLOURS, THEY CAN ALSO BE REALIZED WHEN DIFFERENT TONES FROM THE SAME COLOUR RANGE ARE COMBINED, AS ILLUSTRATED IN THIS DARING, YET SUBTLE, SCHEME.

When done well, combinations based on different tones of one colour can go far beyond simple, graded tints to become a symphony of colours which harmonize with and subtly complement each other.

This apartment in the Scottish city of Glasgow is lucky to have huge windows, and the owner took the exciting and rather brave decision to take advantage of so much natural light and to use colour that in less confident hands might have been thought of as too dark and light-absorbing.

In the living area, over one wall, wide, horizontal bands of deep rich colour are painted – five different colours in actuality: pumpkin orange, gloss black, slate, chocolate and gloss

burgundy; the inspiration for the particular shades coming from the pages of an enamel and car-paint catalogue. Dark and darker, each is different but with underlying similarities, each shade imperceptibly merging into the next without drama. There are no strong contrasts and, though immensely sophisticated, the arrangement gives a warm, comfortable sensation, the overall impression being that of a rich patterned velvet – designed by Fortuny perhaps.

These are the colours of autumn and winter, of earth and harvests – aubergine, hazelnuts and Chinese lanterns. All the shades have black or brown as the underlying colour and,

ABOVE Even the bookshelves in this apartment are incorporated into the warm blend of colours. This shelf, which is used to display a collection of classically modern Keith Murray ceramics, has been painted a rusty orange and stands against a dark-brown wall, the tone of which has been taken from the colour palette featured on the wall of broad stripes.
BELOW In the living room, continuing the theme of seasonal colours, the curtains are made in two separate shades of green – one of deep olive and one of paler lime. A light lime-coloured lamp highlights the contrast.

RIGHT The long wall in the living room has been painted in generously proportioned, over-wide horizontal bands of striking dark, rich colour. The general rule when using colours in a room – but especially when using dark colours – is that the darker colours should be closest to floor level, with the brighter, lighter colours closest to the ceiling. Although here each colour is different, there is a tonal harmony between them that overrides any contrasts.

although they are satisfying together, they need, in order to stand out, a sharp accent to provide contrast and bite. This has been achieved by using orange as the colour nearest to the ceiling. The intelligent positioning of this broad, bright band carries the eye upwards and opens out the room.

The width of the different bands of colour is important – too narrow would be overly busy and would distract the eye from the overall effect. The greater the expanse of wall, the wider the bands of colour should be. It is, as so often, a question of proportion, for it is that which gives harmony to a scheme.

If you want to combine colours as closely in tune as these are, then texture and finish are the elements which will make the difference between the boring and the breathtaking. Were all these colours to be applied in the same finish – flat matt or high gloss, for example – the result would be very different, and not pleasing to the eye. But instead, the difference in finish supplies contrasting texture and adds a tension between the colours as the eye travels from glossy to matt as well as from one subtle tone to another. At the tall wide windows, the curtains are green in two different shades – one olive toned, one lime – thus continuing the idea of tone on tone running through the whole space.

Such a definite colour statement needs decorative details that do not detract from the subtle whole, and any accessories must be carefully chosen. Here it is simple design in the form of a twentieth-century ceramic collection in sculptural shapes, many of them designed by Keith Murray, known for the clean lines of his designs.

LEFT The broad stripes of colour on the wall, the low, long wooden unit, the clean lines of the twentieth-century ceramics and the polished wooden floor all combine to make a most dramatic setting. Many people would have been content with using subtle colours and shapes in this manner, but there are two further touches which take this colour feast an inspiration beyond. One is the visual surprise of having such a bright band of clear orange immediately below the ceiling; the other is the constant contrast in texture and finish — from flat matt to shiny gloss and metallic lustre, the eye is constantly taken by surprise.

Throughout the apartment nothing jars; the colours change, merging from one into the next, but the palette remains the same.

ABOVE Forget the advice always to paint hallways in bright welcoming colours — this hall is dramatic and mysterious … and painted matt black. Even more perverse, the woodwork is painted in a glossy black finish rather than the more usual contrasting colour. But there is another unusual aspect to this matt-black scheme — the paint is made for blackboards, and as such has a practical as well as a decorative aspect.

LEFT Not only the walls but also the windows are graded in bands of colour; behind the dark-toned sofa are hung curtains made in two different shades of green — olive and lime.

Soft simplicity

THE ARTS AND CRAFTS MOVEMENT AROSE, TOWARDS THE END OF THE NINETEENTH CENTURY, FROM A DESIRE BY DESIGNERS AND ARTISTS TO RETURN TO WHAT WAS SEEN AS THE PURE AND THE REAL, AWAY FROM THE OVER-EGGED, OVER-PRODUCED PUDDING OF VICTORIAN TASTE.

The designers and artists who followed Arts and Crafts principles promoted, as well as a much simpler style of design, a completely new field of soft deep colours, which was very far from the garish hues produced with the chemical pigments so loved by the Victorians. These were colours that seemed to come from the woods and fields. They included a deep sage green, a dark red, a teal blue and a brownish purple, often combined with black.

Andrew Wallace is an artist, and in his London apartment many of the colours, as well as some of the internal architecture, are reminiscent of the Arts and Crafts movement, crossed perhaps with the tones of a seventeenth-century Dutch painting, as well as the colours the nineteenth-century Shakers developed from natural pigments. The result in Wallace's capable hands is one of naturalness of tone, of an

ABOVE LEFT Every room is a palette of muted harmonies. These soft, almost rubbed, colours slide easily from room to room – here the soft blue-pink walls, framed with grey-blue woodwork, merge easily into the pale yellow walls and sage-green wood of the kitchen.
LEFT A colour that is almost indescribable covers the walls – the colour of a fading lilac flower perhaps, or of milky drinking chocolate. Many would have used a bright colour on the woodwork, but the pale blue-grey tones that Andrew Wallace has used to outline the windows are far more subtle.

earthy quality, and a softness of hue. Throughout the apartment there are unexpected colour combinations. Wallace's colours are cool, and in each of them – even the yellow – there is a hint, a touch, even the faintest idea, of blue or grey. This colour connection means that all the combinations work perfectly, contrasting but never clashing. Nothing is glossy or glittery; everything, whether woodwork or walls, is flat and soft, often giving an almost velvety appearance.

A colour has little or no meaning on its own. It is only when it is set against another colour or colours, when thought has been given as to how the different shades or hues will work together, that you produce a scheme with any depth. When using colour in a relatively small space, it is vital that harmony is present, that each area, each room, links with what is around it, as well as the colour of the adjoining space. Here, even the varying colours of the woodwork in each room are carefully chosen to act as a frame for other colours present, working together with an indefinable charm. It is a lesson in using colour. But then from an artist you would expect nothing less.

LEFT A detail that could come straight out of an American Shaker home, where practicality and function – beauty through simplicity with no unnecessary ornament – were the aims, and colours were made from natural ingredients. These baskets, used as instant storage and hung by hooks from the low windowsill, become decoration in its purest form. The glow of the red apples highlights and emphasizes the flat tones surrounding the baskets.

ABOVE Rubbed maize-yellow walls are a background for watered Wedgwood windows and sage-green cupboards, and the stripped, original parquet floor becomes part of the same soft palette. Every surface is powdered and soft, except the polished pots and pans.

Throughout the house, the woodwork is a soft blue-green, sometimes combined with blues and sometimes with yellow. In the central hall, three wooden chairs sit, like a group of sunning holidaymakers. The arrangement looks informal but is actually carefully worked out.

Each a slightly different colour and shape, they are transformed into a group with the aid of the pictures arranged above them on a yellow wall. The woodwork echoes the colour of the chairs and again pulls the seating together.

Ice-cream cool

LIKE ITALIAN ICE CREAM, ALL THE COLOURS IN THIS COUNTRY HOUSE LOOK AS IF THEY SHOULD BE SCOOPED OUT OF TUBS AND OFFERED IN CONES. AND IN EACH GROUPING, AMONGST THE COOL, PALE COLOURS, THERE IS ALWAYS A DASH OF ASTRINGENCY – A SLIGHTLY SHARPER TONE.

Although it is not always considered, appropriateness – the sense of place – is all-important in choosing which colours to use in a house. No matter how perfectly conceived the scheme, how sympathetic the colours, or how carefully chosen the tints and shades, if the colour combinations and finishes are not sympathetic to the architecture, the scheme will fail miserably. In this pretty, converted byre in the English countryside, designed and decorated by Nicholas and Vanessa Arbuthnot, a neoclassical scheme, for example – all black and gilding and Pompeian red – would have been ludicrously misplaced. An extreme example perhaps, but one that makes the point.

But as it is, this house is a miracle of appropriateness: all the colours are light and fresh – the sort of colours that used to be called pastel, but without the slightly insipid connotations that that word sometimes holds. Most of the wood, including furniture and floors, has been painted and colour-washed – much of it a cool duck-egg blue – and this is an integral part of the overall scheme. Too often the colour opportunities offered by woodwork are thrown away or ignored, but this colourist embraces the opportunity with enthusiasm. Coloured woodwork can be used as punctuation – a gentle comma or a sharp full stop. It can be used to emphasize or accentuate, and it can be used to ground a scheme and soften it. It can also play an important role in changing architectural perceptions.

ABOVE LEFT In one, huge open-plan room, which combines the kitchen with a living, relaxing and eating space, the same blue-green woodwork that is found in the rest of the house pulls the look together. Clear yellow walls ('Hay' by Farrow and Ball) are the background for different blue and green combinations, from the blue check cloth to the painted wooden chairs and the ubiquitous woodwork.
LEFT Here an astringent touch of brighter colour is used to stop the ice-cream colours from becoming saccharine. A wooden day-bed is covered in a red-and-white check blanket, and the curtains are made from a white and peony-red ticking.

LEFT Another example of nature's colour sense: these roses, whilst quite different in hue, are each of similar strength and depth, and so go perfectly together. They illustrate just how much inspiration for colour schemes can be picked from the garden. The Arbuthnots have used this natural lesson in all the colours throughout the house, which is particularly important as the garden seems almost to be part of every room, flooding in through open doors and windows.

Using pale colours together in a house is a bit like dressing all in pale colours. It works when the colours are in the similar tones and have the same depth to them; so pale blue, pale pink and pale lilac will work together without trouble, although they may need to be rescued from insipidity with a bright accent – a sharp red, a bright yellow – or a flash of white to pull them together. And, although they should all be equally cold or warm, there must be some variation – some of the tones should be slightly deeper or darker, lighter or paler.

Here, there is nothing insipid, nothing dull – all is sunny, accessible and uplifting.

It looks simple, but in fact using these faux-naïve colours requires a confidence and discipline of choice. The colours here – mostly cool and pale – have been used in ravishing combinations that never slide into the naïve or the dull. The colour palette is almost Scandinavian – or what people often think of as Scandinavian – cool pale blues and blue-greens flow over the walls, floors and furniture. The sympathetic furnishings are mostly checks and stripes in clear pinks and blues. The necessary astringent touch is provided by the odd yellow and red, which makes it all so much more complex an idea.

Using a fairly limited palette means that there is harmony from space to space, and through each door the next area beckons. Spatial harmony is doubly important in a house where the outside is brought inside through numerous French windows. This is a proper country house and the colours that are used reinforce this feeling.

LEFT The living end of the large all-purpose room is an area of comfort and leisure, suggested not only by the continued use of the same soft ice-cream colour but also by the softening effect of the textiles used on the table and day-bed. It is interesting how many patterns have been used together; because they are largely geometric, there is no conflict of design.

RIGHT An Aga, particularly an original model such as this, will always hold centre stage, and here a definite effort has been made to work the woodwork in with the cream-coloured beast.

BELOW A small, awkwardly shaped bedroom in the eaves has been given the toning neutral treatment, with walls and wooden bed painted in a soft stone colour, and the eaves and beams painted in white. So that the scheme does not disappear into neutrality, the night table is little-girl pink and cushions on the bed are in assorted pink tones and patterns.

THIS PAGE In the living area of this small and shiny space, the walls have been coloured by rubbing purple pigment into the wet plaster. The result is a rich, varied finish with depth and subtle tones, reminiscent of deep-pile velvet. A bench cut out of the wall and covered in bright orange divides the living space from the kitchen area.

Sharp contrast

IT MAY SEEM OBVIOUS, BUT THE COLOURS THAT YOU CHOOSE TO HAVE AROUND YOU SHOULD BE THOSE THAT SUIT YOUR TEMPERAMENT. ALTHOUGH MANY PEOPLE PROFESS TO LIKE BRIGHT COLOURS AND TO FIND THEM CHEERFUL, NOT EVERYONE CAN ACTUALLY LIVE WITH THEM; SOME PEOPLE ARE SIMPLY HAPPIER WITH MUTED TONES.

For the many who do love bright tones, using them in combination with each other can produce the most stimulating schemes and original rooms. Because of their strength, bright colours cannot simply be mixed together in any old way; success comes either by building a scheme around one strong tone with sharp contrasts or by taking a family of colours and using them in all their variations. The apartment on these pages – small and compact but with plentiful natural light – brilliantly demonstrates the use of colour in a limited space.

Secondary colours are, generally speaking, easier to use than primaries; they are not as intense and have a little more subtlety. In this apartment, purple is the starring secondary – it purrs and hums and all other colours defer to it. In some areas, many tones of purple are used together, from deep blue-purple to lilac. Elsewhere there is contrast: sharp yellows, pinks and oranges highlight and accent. These colours work in this role because yellow, pink and orange are themselves interdependent – part of a group sitting adjacent to each other on the colour wheel – and so work together without fighting.

Throughout the apartment, whenever a bright colour is used, it is softened by being set against a dark one: bright acid pink against dark blue on the cupboards or against a wall built up from layers of blue and purple. In all, an astonishing total of fourteen colours have been used in an instructive display of disciplined bravura.

LEFT A detail of the plaster finish of the living area walls; the tones of the wall are emphasized by the carmine pink shelf and the softer blue-purple cupboard doors. In a space which is as small as this, it is important to pay close attention to detail. Every surface should be considered.
TOP In the kitchen, the most unusual materials – as well as colours – have been used. Wall cupboards are faced in perforated metal and hung above a reflective splash-back made from mirrored glass, which adds a sense of space. Against the mirrors is a vibrant pink worktop, which contrasts with dark grey-painted kitchen cupboards.

ABOVE Dividing the living area from the kitchen is a pillar unit in purple faced in yellow, which leads the eye to the kitchen beyond. Pink chairs make a connection with the bright pink worktop.

ROBERT MORRIS

The Tate Gallery

Colours to transform

Colour is subjective – no two people see any one colour in the same way. However, there are some basic principles which mean that colour can be used to hide, disguise, deceive and repair. For this reason, it is an important weapon in the armoury of interior design.

Not many rooms are perfect; in fact most rooms have their share of imperfections, be it the shape or size of the space, or the quality of light. However, much can be done both to disguise and to visually correct them, with the judicious use of clever colouring. We all know that strong colour draws the eye inwards, and that light colour moves the eye away. This means that, in a relatively uncluttered space, the right use of colour can be used to accentuate one feature and minimize another, with accents of other colours used as punctuation marks within the total plan.

Colour can work in several different ways: by visually accentuating or diminishing an architectural flaw or flaws; by suggesting partitions and demarcation lines; or by altering the atmosphere of a room through the suggestion of a function or a mood.

One of the best pieces of advice that an interior designer or decorator can give is that, in general terms, it is better by far to have one good idea and be able to follow it through boldly than to have several quite good ideas, none of which are executed with complete confidence and clarity. And this rule applies particularly where colour is concerned. Colour is there to be looked at – it is the first thing one notices about a room. Therefore, when colour is being used to say something – to convey an idea or a mood, or to delineate an area or a space – it is important that it is allowed to speak with a clear and confident voice. Likewise, colours used for this purpose should not be presented in a confused or overcrowded way – they should be allowed to make their points, and do the work that you are asking of them.

OPPOSITE When black and white are used together in this way, they become colours as opinionated and as strong as any others. A third colour introduced into the equation – in this case an exuberant green-tendrilled plant – automatically emphasizes the contrast between the other two.
PREVIOUS PAGE The most confident colour combination of all is probably red, black and white, particularly when all are presented in a high-shine gloss. Each element in this room makes its point – in a particularly strong and telling way.

Colour zoning

COLOUR IS A DECORATIVE TOOL IN SEVERAL WAYS: IT CAN BE USED NOT ONLY TO BRING INTEREST, WARMTH, LIGHT AND MOOD TO A ROOM, BUT IT CAN ALSO WORK TOWARDS MORE TANGIBLE, PRACTICAL PURPOSES, SUCH AS THE DELINEATION AND DIVISION OF SPACE AND FUNCTION.

Colour can be a powerful weapon when used to define and mark out space. Once again, the work of the legendary Mexican architect, Luis Barragán is called to mind. As Barragán's designs illustrated so forcefully, flat planes of colour can break up a space as effectively as any solid, closed door. Colour used thus should contrast or complement – what is most important is that the colours, when seen together, should work in harmony. When you look through one room into another, or from a hall or passage, you should feel a sense of calm and of place – of one space leading effortlessly into another.

Once houses were always designed as whole spaces – to be looked on in their entirety. But modern conversions of large areas into smaller ones, including apartments designed for open-plan living, mean that many homes have architectural or design anomalies. Such anomalies, whether structural or decorative, can

On one wall of the living area, shades of yellow, ranging from bright to light, subtly colour and break up the extended space of this city loft apartment. Everything is integral to the final effect, including the chairs, almost sculptural objects in their own right, and even the cushions and throws used with them. Sand-blasted glass – although not technically a colour – is also used in the design plan as a surface and a divider, as well as providing another change in tonal definition across the space.

FAR LEFT In the enclosed but open kitchen space, the appliances seem to float in a sea of glossy red. A respite from the density of colour on the wall and worktop has been achieved by seemingly random shapes impressed into the surface. The compact wooden kitchen table tucked behind a pier and the open-work metal chair also serve to break up the space.

LEFT The accent colour – not an obvious choice at first sight – is blue, ranging in shade from pale to bright, and is used throughout the space.

often be absorbed with correct colour use. It is useful, rather than looking for problems on a room-to-room or corner-to-corner level, first to look at the area in total. Sometimes a problem in a room seems to resolve itself when you work on the whole space rather than the specific.

The oversized loft apartment, seen on these pages, illustrates this perfectly. Here, colour is efficiently and cleverly used to delineate space and function whilst also being part of a sophisticated colour scheme that pleases the eye on more than one level. In the living area of the apartment, yellow is used, in all its variants, as the unifying tone, whilst the kitchen area, which leads directly from it, is shiny red broken with sand-blasted glass and raw brickwork. Accents of blue – from the pale blue-grey of the glass dividers to the warm tones of the kitchenware – are used in small doses throughout the apartment, linking the bright red, clear yellow and orange.

LEFT Nature rarely gets it wrong, so never dismiss natural colour combinations out of hand: these long-stemmed anemones with their deep-red petals and a contrasting central circle of powdery black stamens, illustrate how to break up harmoniously an area of colour with the addition of a sharp accent in an equally strong tone.

ABOVE RIGHT The natural notion illustrated in the anemones has been reproduced in the kitchen by adding a cutting

edge of black to both the cabinets and the geometric lines of the painted window frames.

RIGHT Although it is fun and stimulating to use bright colours together, it is important to know when to stop. Here, outside the actual

cooking area and against a sand-blasted glass dividing panel, the dining table, its matching high-backed chairs and even the low-level hanging lights are as neutral as the glass and so provide a cool, harmonious link.

Planes of colour demarcate space and function, while maintaining a harmony throughout the apartment.

Shaping a space with colour is as much to do with creating a mood as with architectural precepts. It is always important that there is enough of the dominant colour to make the point, but not so much that it is uncomfortable to live in. Nearly all colours need contrasts and accents of other colours or textures. You may expect red to be overpowering and too 'hot' in the kitchen. But, when combined with a large space, it proves to be energizing and stimulating. It gives – perhaps surprisingly – an air of efficiency, whilst also being a good background against which to eat.

In the converted school space seen here, architect Voon Wong has employed the same principles but with an altogether quieter, more subtle palette. A single, relatively small, but high-ceilinged room has been masterly converted into a spacious apartment, which

OPPOSITE On the walls of the central living area, a pale mushroom colour predominates and leads around the corner to a wall of dark air-force blue-grey that delineates the eating area.
LEFT Against the end wall, a bench covered in suede is trimmed with an orange metal strip. The simple wooden table with grey legs is reflected in the glossy dark-grey floor.
ABOVE Colour is used here to make sure that there is no jarring of tones. The sofa against the mushroom wall is upholstered in cream; the cushions are in tones of blues, browns and creams, both plain and striped; the stool is ceramic, glazed cream; and even the cup is matt, dark brown.

holds – as well as a comfortable living area – a kitchen suspended from the floor and a mezzanine space hung from the ceiling that incorporates both bedroom and office. A deep-blue entrance hall is echoed by the slightly softer blue of the rear wall. Elsewhere, grey, white, cream and mushroom work in balance and harmony, leading the eye and pointing out the perimeters of each area. Light floods through the two huge windows, and the intelligent architectural solutions to turning a Victorian workplace into a contemporary living and working space are emphasized by the never emphatic, but always appropriate, palette.

Many of the larger spaces that are now subdivided were once nineteenth-century warehouses, industrial buildings or, as in this case, schools. Because of their size, these are precisely the sort of spaces that benefit

THIS PAGE An overview of Voon Wong's apartment shows not only the lower living area but also the mezzanine floor which holds the architectural studio as well as, behind the Venetian-blinded window, the bedroom. The internal window means that as much light as possible reaches the bedroom area, and also that curtains or blinds are not needed at the original, oversized windows. The floor, which is the old school parquet, damaged by time and use, has been transformed by being painted a very glossy dark grey; it acts as a strong and cohesive link throughout the apartment.

RIGHT One side of the small, cleverly designed open kitchen is built against a conventional wall; the other is suspended from the mezzanine ceiling so that the floor area is not broken up unnecessarily.
BELOW The small bedroom is simplicity itself, with a low bed dressed in white against white walls and a mouse-grey carpet. Natural light is diffused through the silver-white Venetian blinds. In the wall opposite the bed, a shallow shelf unit has been made with a recessed television slotted into it. The unit is painted in soothing grey-lilac.

best from colour used in an architectural manner. When industrial spaces were first converted, they were often painted white, to emphasize the feeling of unaccustomed space. But colour works better in an open space, adding personality and presence.

Colour used to accentuate or 'mark out' can be strong or it can be subtle and soft – it is the idea of the colour making the design points that is important, not the tones themselves. When colour is used in this almost mathematical way, the art is to choose tones and shades that work together, that are part of a recognizable palette, yet have enough contrast within that group. The eye must be guided harmoniously and without protest around the space. Nothing must shout, and yet nothing must bore. A counsel of perfection might be to ensure that every other element in the space is also within the same palette, with just a few shots of contrasting colour.

Making shapes

THE POWER OF COLOURS TO ADVANCE OR GUIDE, TO
RETREAT OR BE NEUTRAL IS BOUNDLESS. IF WE WANT
TO EMPHASIZE SPECIAL FEATURES, TO GIVE PROMINENCE
TO A PROJECTION, TO DEEPEN A HOLLOW OR TO CORRECT
ARCHITECTURAL FAULTS, THE CLEVER EMPLOYMENT OF
THIS POWER CAN BE OF THE GREATEST ASSISTANCE.

With just a little thought, colouring can be used to transform awkward spaces. There are various colour constants which can be employed on specific problems. Bright light colour, for example, will open up a space and give a new prominence to objects and furniture. Generally speaking, whites, purer yellows and light pinks have the property of advancing and giving prominence to areas and objects. Greens and blues make objects recede and become less important, whilst reds – as long as they are judiciously used – are of neutral or intermediate influence.

In a small, low room, a bright light colour on the ceiling will extend the room upwards, and the same sort of colour – best used in a glossy finish – will tend to push the walls outwards. Whites, creams, yellows and pale reds all reflect light and would, in most cases, be more effective than duller colours, such as pale greys or browns.

If a room is of irregular shape – perhaps widening at one end, or with walls that slope inwards to the ceiling, or have other awkward angles – then use only one light colour over everything, and avoid eye-distracting contrasts.

Colours that reflect light tend to give a cheerful appearance. Too often an overly dark room is synonymous with gloom – applying a bright light colour to the walls will change that. A cold room will benefit not only from a warm colour on the walls but also from warmth in textile colour, adding texture to the complete scheme.

Should a room be too large – it can happen – a dark colour on the ceiling will push the ceiling downwards. If the ceiling colour is painted right down to the picture rail, this feeling will be emphasized. Darker colour on the walls will create the illusion of bringing them together; a subtle effect can be achieved by colouring two facing walls

THIS PAGE Artist Andrew Wallace has made a sparkling virtue of his internal, windowless corridor by transforming it into a tale of carefully chosen and combined colour that invites close inspection. The walls have been painted an Arts and Crafts 'greenery-yallery', which contrasts with yellow-toned dark green glossy woodwork. The ceiling is false – the original ceilings throughout the apartment were a restorer's nightmare, so Wallace took a lateral view and built new hand-cut wooden ones on top of the old; the hall ceiling is painted dark brick red with deep green beams, decorated in almost Gothic style within the panels. The final effect is totally pleasing, and the contrast of the surprising, dark ceiling and lighter walls gives the corridor an illusion of width.

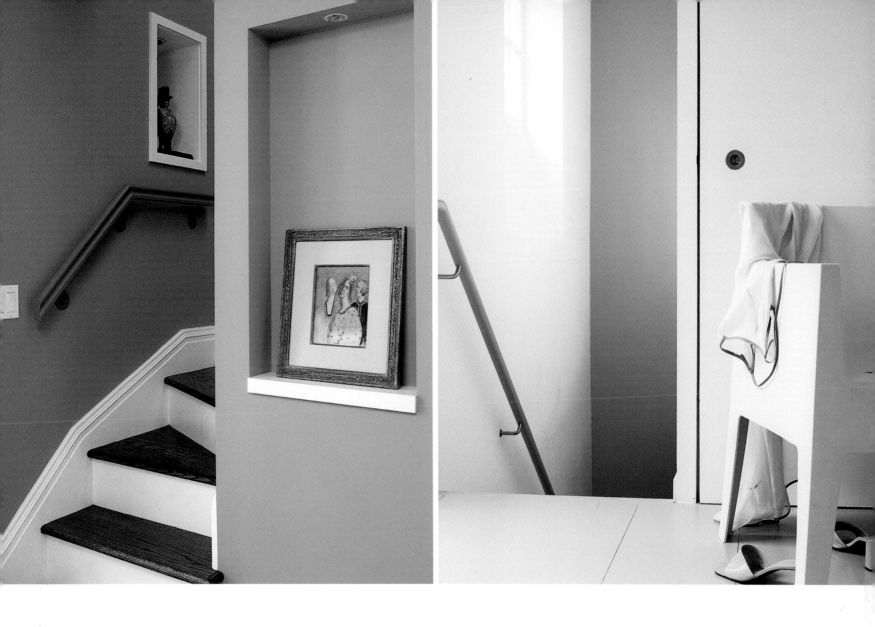

THIS PAGE In this small studio house, most of the colours are pale and neutral, so the apple green on the staircase comes as a surprise — a welcome one, of course. It is used as a zone maker as well as a decorative contrast, and acts first as a marker — a signpost showing the way as it leads down from the bedroom, which is a symphony in greys and blues, and connects it with the other parts of the house. It also adds a relaxing, soft tone to an otherwise cool environment. Fresh and clean, the green makes the white surroundings sing, and it acts as a strong background colour to the pictures and objects that are displayed.

RIGHT In this converted barn, close to the sea and marshland, a small bedroom has been carved out of the eaves; the contrast of such fresh blue and such clear white gives the space a feeling that is far from claustrophobia.

BELOW On the lower level of the barn, the blue walls change in tone and depth as the light hits them; the undulating curve of the surface accentuates these changes, and is itself an echo of the changing sea.

BOTTOM Blue is not the only colour used in the barn: another sea colour, green – the green of water close to the shore, and water over pebbles – has also been employed. Although they are perhaps not what might be termed sophisticated or 'city' shades, together the two watery tones work in harmony, defining and linking the spaces, and altering as they are touched by the ever-changing seaside light.

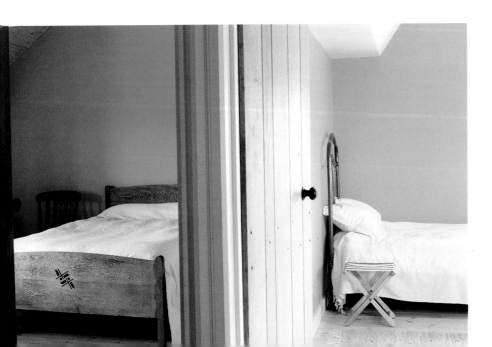

Colours can have an important architectural role in changing spaces and they can, at the same time, make a room feel instantly cheerful or gloomy.

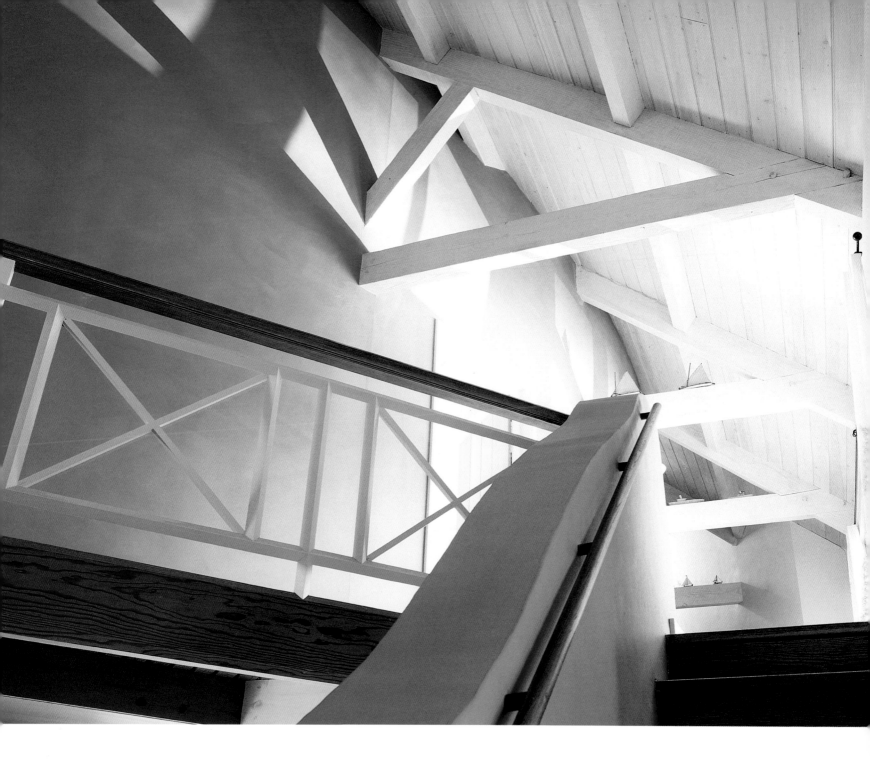

with one shade, and a slightly deeper variation of the same colour on the opposing walls. Dark reds, browns, greens and blues absorb light and so will darken a room and, if the texture of the colour is matt, light will be further absorbed.

Although, for this reason, dark colours are usually used in lighter spaces, there is an argument for emphasizing the confines of a space with dark strong, contrasting colour, and conventional narrow entrance halls are good areas for such experimentation. The fact that the area available for using colour in the hall

and up the staircase is so limited, and the walls and woodwork are in such close proximity to each other, means that you have the opportunity to try out all those unusual combinations that might be too much over a larger area. Think shocking pink with forest green or deep purple; mandarin orange with electric blue; or saffron yellow with terracotta. The one stipulation is that any colour chosen – for the wall, at any rate – should be warm in tone – the hall is a place of first impressions, which should, of course, always be good.

THIS PAGE In the same converted barn, made of brick and flint, colour has been used both to open up spaces and to mark out areas. Here, different shades of blue have been used in what might be described as architectural fashion, to work together but also to point out different functions – the stair rail up a wooden staircase; an upper wall leading to bedrooms. Significantly, blue is also used to underline the geographical situation of sea and sky.

BELOW AND LEFT Now that it is no longer considered necessary that every bathroom should look like the inside of a fridge – and usually feel like one, too – colour can be employed in this bastion of gentle hedonism. The smaller the room, the warmer the colour. Amaryllis red is the tone used in this bathroom, a velvety soft red which gives an instant air of warmth and comfort. In an interesting contrast, the softness of the colour is lifted and sharpened by being paired with a beaten metal basin and a wooden-framed circular mirror.

RIGHT AND FAR RIGHT This warm red living room is exotic and – rather surprisingly – calm, as well. The owner-designer achieved the effect by first colouring the walls with a matt, rich red pigment, and then glazing the base colour with a dark red glaze. The finished effect is warm but saved from all-pervasive richness by the clean and most satisfying contrast of the furnishings.

Creating atmosphere

USING COLOUR TO TRANSFORM IS NOT ONLY A QUESTION
OF WHAT YOU WANT TO CHANGE ABOUT THE SHAPE OR
ASPECT OF THE SPACE ITSELF — COLOUR CAN TRANSFORM
FUNCTION AND MOOD AS WELL AS ARCHITECTURAL FAULTS.

Psychological, as well as optical, illusions can be
performed with colour. The atmosphere of a room can
be enhanced or even transformed by the judicious use
of the right tones on the walls and furnishings.

This transformation can be engineered by utilizing
people's known reactions to specific colours: we know,
for example, that green – soft green, anyway – is a
soothing colour, so we expect, when we see it on the
walls of a room, that everything will quietly blend in
and that we will feel soothed. The only problem with
this thesis is that many relatively soft greens are not
soothing it all – if they have too much yellow in them,
they can appear positively bilious; the lesson being
that careful choice is essential if you want to use
colour in this way.

One must also consider the uses and purpose of
the room under discussion. Different rooms respond
to different types of colour. Bedrooms should, on the
whole, be coloured in soft tones; kitchens and dining
rooms in cheerful, welcoming colours that are
conducive to eating and hospitality; and sitting rooms
– well they should be whatever suits the function
of the room, whether it is a place of entertainment,

THIS PAGE Throughout this London apartment, grey tones colour the greens and blues, the total effect being a soft impression of everyday London life – but an impression far more pleasant than the chilliness encountered on the average winter's day outside. Inside the apartment, the rooms look as if an opaque film has been lifted from the colours of the everyday world – the greens are crisper, the blues softer, and the greys clearer.

a place of family relaxation, or a combination of the two.

A rich red living room can be warm and exotic, but can also feel oppressive and overpowering. Not every room – or every homeowner – is suited to strong colour, and many people seek a more subtle and soothing effect when choosing their palette. Nothing could be a greater contrast to the richness of the living room on the previous page than the pale colours of the apartment shown here. Again, natural lighting has played a prominent role in the colour selection. The idea behind the decorative scheme of this London apartment was to echo and complement the natural – often grey – tones of the English winter light, so the colour scheme is cool, understandably, but also calm and ordered, a combination of colour and texture.

The aspect of the room is always an important consideration when choosing colours, but is especially so when the creation of a mood is the purpose. In

Colour should always be used in conjunction with lighting, for colour can not give light, only reflect it.

a dark room, or where the desired effect is to be dark and rich, colour should always be used in conjunction with lighting. Well-placed lamps and background lighting can completely alter a room. Light is reflected differently off different-coloured surfaces, so tones and shades of colour should be chosen taking into account not only the size and shape of the room and its aspect, but also other less obvious, external factors, such as the proximity of buildings and trees reflecting light through the windows.

This north-facing bedroom is coloured in tones of soft blue-greys and whites. Pale blue-grey walls, and a painted grey wooden floor are the background for an aluminium bedside table. The bed-linen is pale striped grey, and the chair is painted in the palest of grey tones. Considering the direction in which the room faces, this is a colour combination that could be too cold; the fact that it works says much for the subtlety of each tone.

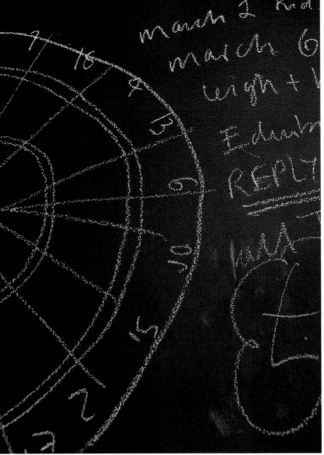

THIS PAGE Many specialist paints made commercially can be used in a domestic context; blackboard paint is an obvious example. Instead of using it on a portable blackboard, why not use it, as here, to cover a whole wall – or walls. Pictured is a small, already dark hallway, where the bonus of a wraparound blackboard so near the front door can be easily appreciated.
OPPOSITE This striking, dramatic effect proves that 'keep it simple' applies in more areas than cookery. But, although a simple idea and design, there is a sophistication in the choice of textures, where matt and gloss finishes and metallic paint – another specialist product – have been included.

Colour techniques

Colour techniques – by which one means the craft of applying colour to surfaces in a way that enhances both the former and the latter – are the oldest tricks in the painting book. Ever since man first discovered colour, he has been experimenting with different ways of decorating with it. Applying it in multicoloured layers, combing, ragging, sponging, dragging it – his inventiveness knew no bounds. And today we are once again fascinated with this decorative art, fascinated with creating texture and pattern, with bestowing instant age and patination on a surface, with covering it in designs that are regular in content or loose and free-flowing.

The methods at their most basic are just that, and can be easily learned. There are, of course, some techniques that require the skilled hand of an artist, but then there is, after all, an artist in everybody. It is a question of practice and confidence. And, even if you need the help of a professional in translating your ideas into reality, the pleasure that comes from discussing the colours and the design, watching it take shape and admiring the finished result, can be huge indeed. The joy of using any of these finishes on what would otherwise be a plain wall or object is that the end result will be something completely individual and unique.

Unusual finishes

BECAUSE SUCH A WIDE RANGE OF COMMERCIAL PAINT IS
EASILY AVAILABLE TODAY, YOU MIGHT THINK THAT THE BEST
WAY TO GET THE SUBTLE, INTERESTING COLOUR YOU ARE
LOOKING FOR WOULD BE SIMPLY TO BUY THE RIGHT TIN OF
PAINT AND SLAP IT ON THE WALL. HOWEVER, A DECORATOR
OR INTERIOR DESIGNER WOULD BEG TO DIFFER.

What some would call a 'mechanical' finish has always
been an anathema to decorators and taste makers. He
or she would, in most cases, consider modern paints
to be a trifle too plastic, lacking depth and subtlety.
And, useful as commercial paints are in many areas,
there are some situations or decorative schemes where
a slightly more individual treatment is required.

Such individuality could be achieved perhaps by
using one of the many specialist paints now available,
which include many once-rare traditional natural
paints. Lime washes, distempers and milk paints –
evocative names for those interested in the history of
decoration – are paints which, when applied, display
soft, almost organic surfaces. Lime washes, for
example, are organic and were traditionally used to
paint exteriors; they breathe, wear gently over the years
and allow moisture to pass through. And distemper,
the traditional interior paint to be used over plaster,
has a cloudy, slightly powdery, subtle finish.

Alternatively, individuality could be acquired with
one of the range of new colour exotica. Paint that
glitters, glow-in-the-dark paint and fluorescent paint
are all now available from large suppliers. Metallic
paints, too, which were once only produced by
specialist makers, can be easily found in a wide range
of finishes: from white-gold and burnished gold to soft
verdigris and burnished bronze; from antique copper
to frosted silver. Even a touch of one of these could
add instant interest to an unprepossessing space.

For many hundreds of years, of course, colour was
brought into a room and onto the walls by hanging real
textiles. Sometimes they were portable, like tapestries,
and sometimes they were permanent. Like all the best
decorative ideas, wall-hung textiles have never really

ABOVE AND BELOW Gold leaf is one
of the most beautiful – and
expensive – finishes that there is.
Redolent of luxury – Renaissance
grandeur and eighteenth-century
beauty – few people employ it as a
wall finish today. But here, in a
Milanese dining room, it is used to
great effect. The entire wall is gold
leaf, except for an arched area
which has been painted in deep
turquoise and hung with a
collection of plates that follow the
golden curve. Below the turquoise
section, paintings are hung almost
to floor level. The effect is
overwhelmingly rich. The detail
shows how small each leaf is and
how many are needed to cover even
the smallest of areas.

gone away. In France, for example, textiles – often highly patterned like the toile de Jouy or the bright Provençal naïve patterns – are often hung, particularly in bedrooms. Textiles on walls give a completely different texture from paper or paint, no matter how well printed or applied. First, because the walls are usually lined, a material-hung room has a warmth and a softness to it that is inimitable; second, the natural flaws in the weave mean that, even if in a plain weave, there is a variety and texture apparent in every metre; and third, light strikes textiles in a different, subtle way, so that each wall looks quite different.

Textiles can be hung in panels, combined with paint or paper or, reverting to the style of the Middle Ages, they can be loosely hung against the wall or even from a rail or pole around the wall to fall to ground level like a curtain. One decorator has attached short lengths of curtain pole on different walls of her sitting room and routinely hangs an ever-changing library of panels of material to add instant colour and design to the room. The secret here is to vary the textiles in an unusual way – perhaps a deep-red silk damask might be hung next to a pink and green document chintz and a pale-green and gold sari length.

THIS PAGE Some decorators – particularly in Europe – think of textiles as a possible wall covering before they consider paper or paint. The advantages are apparent in the range of texture and tone offered by a fabric-hung wall. The owner of this Paris apartment *(right and below)* appreciates the variety of textiles and has used them severally. In the bedroom, a matt raspberry-toned textile makes a suitably warm atmosphere; and in the drawing room the walls are covered in the same green velvet as the adjacent curtains. In contemporary contrast, the walls of a cloakroom in Manhattan *(below left)* are covered with silk in hazelnut tones with a muted variegated stripe.

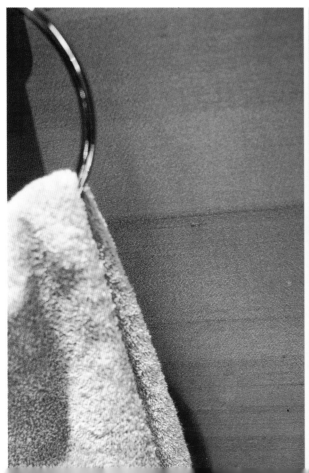

THIS PAGE The joy of using colour washes and glazes is that you can eventually build up any depth of any colour that you want, with as much texture and subtlety as is required. The best examples no longer look like pigmented colour painted in layers onto a plaster surface; they resemble almost anything else that is beautiful – the celadon glaze on a piece of antique porcelain, the pile of a rich piece of silk velvet, the subtle melange of colours in a panicle of lilac blossom, or the different tones of a ripening apple. Washes and glazes are infinitely forgiving: the build-up of colour layers can be worked on ad infinitum, 'knocked back' or dirtied until you have exactly the effect that you are looking for.

Washes and glazes

ANOTHER WAY TO ACHIEVE AN INTERESTING FINISH ON THE WALLS IS BY USING ONE OF THE MANY PAINT TECHNIQUES DEVISED OVER THE YEARS. EVER SINCE PIGMENT WAS FIRST USED TO COVER WALL SURFACES (PROBABLY BY THE EARLY EGYPTIANS) PAINTERS HAVE AIMED TO ACHIEVE A SUBTLE EFFECT BY BUILDING UP TRANSPARENT LAYERS OF COLOUR, APPLIED ONE ON TOP OF THE OTHER.

This technique can be called colour-washing, although different specialists give it differing names; it is achieved when one or two thinned coats of colour are applied over a base colour to create a translucent soft effect of colour and tone. The layers applied may be shades of the same colour or carefully chosen combinations of colour, to give subtle effects of tone and shade. The final effect varies considerably according to the materials used and the way the technique is applied, and it can be used on both walls and woodwork to great effect.

There are several methods, depending on whether you are using water- or oil-based paints or tinted glazes. It is best to consult a specialist book on how best to prepare the surface, and mix the pigments depending on your choice of materials. At its simplest, a basic technique using water-based paints to give a wash of colour might consist of a coat of vinyl or acrylic coloured emulsion diluted with water and brushed over a non-porous base coat. The paint should be sufficiently thinned (but not thinned so much that it pours in rivulets onto the ground) to cover the wall quickly, using a wide decorator's brush. The brush should move in wide strokes in every direction and, as the wash begins to dry, it should be brushed again to partly even out the strokes. It must then be left to dry completely, after which another coat – the same colour or perhaps a slightly different tone – can be applied. When applying this second coat, care should be taken to cover any particularly patchy sections of the first coat. The effect will be of soft, shadowy colour and, the more coats you apply, the stronger the colour will be – it's up to you.

The same technique can be used with oil-based paints – diluted with white spirit rather than the water used for emulsion paints. Oil-based paints remain workable for a longer time, giving you more time to execute the brushwork. The paint should be thinned sufficiently to allow you flexibility, and the background kept light. At first, until you are confident about combining colour, it is probably best to keep the colour combinations simple.

A professional decorator would, more than likely, do his colour-washing using a scumble glaze rather than thinned paint. The glaze might be either oil- or acrylic-based and he or she would tint it with artist's pigments or oil paint for the former, and acrylic or water-based paints for the latter. The glaze is thinned – the more solvent you add, the quicker the glaze will dry – and the colour is added. If you are tinting the glaze with artist's pigments, the pigment should be diluted first in white spirit and then stirred into the scumble.

A professional might apply as many as five or six layers of tinted glaze; the subtle, translucent finish of the colours achieved this way produces a colour of depth and subtlety that might look like lacquer or finely glazed porcelain. These glazes dry quite rapidly, so they are not as easy to apply as thinned paints, and the brush strokes must be evenly applied, but the luminosity and depth of colour reward the effort.

ABOVE AND LEFT There is something particularly soothing and effective about a wash or glaze that looks almost like polished raw plaster – which can also be achieved, but which is not always practical if the existing walls are already painted. The muted tones of pinks, creams and browns, worked together and over each other, give a finish that is immensely flattering – as a background for pictures and objects, but also for everyday life.

washes and glazes **181**

Decorative paintwork

IF SOMETHING MORE ELABORATE THAN A COLOUR WASH IS NEEDED, THERE ARE VARIOUS DECORATIVE EFFECTS THAT CAN BE APPLIED, USING TECHNIQUES EITHER TO REMOVE WET PAINT OR TO ADD EXTRA LAYERS FOR TEXTURE AND PATTERN.

Colour washes can be given a variety of different textures and patterns by distressing the surface – either by brushing on or wiping off additional coats. There are a number of tools and techniques for working with the wet surface of the wall; the most popular finishes are probably sponging, stippling, ragging and dragging.

Sponging is one of the easiest of finishes. Over a base colour, watered-down paint or a glaze is either dabbed on with a sponge (sponging on), or – effected in reverse – a fairly fluid layer of colour is painted onto the wall and immediately dabbed off with a sponge and a cloth (sponging off). Using diluted emulsion paints gives a dry, soft effect; oil-based sponging is sharper, and oil glazes give a translucent finish. Real sponges are best, but cellular sponges will work if you rough them up a bit first so that the texture is uneven. Either put the sponge, lightly loaded with paint, onto the wall and dab gently, covering the surface, or apply the coloured paint or glaze first and then, with the sponge wrung out in solvent, dab to lift some of the glaze from the surface. This can be done over several layers of colour.

Stippling is another way to break up the surface in a subtle manner. Usually done using a special brush with a rectangular head, a glaze or wash is applied and then – while still wet – dabbed with the brush so that the colour is lifted, leaving a texture rather

THIS PAGE One of the pleasures of using paint effects is mixing different styles and techniques together. Here, interior designer Geraldine Prieur has combined tone upon tone of colour in different ways: the walls have been washed over a pale pink base and lightly ragged with a darker shade on top; they have then had stripes applied over the wash in a soft, pale melon glaze. The panels of the doors have been painted to resemble watered silk, and the moulding is outlined in two different strong pinks – one deeper than the other.

like shagreen. Stippling can be done successfully on water- and oil-based paints as well as over a tinted scumble glaze.

Rag-rolling and ragging do exactly what they say. The first is achieved by folding a piece of cloth into an even sausage shape and then using it almost like a rolling pin over a wet glazed or painted surface. Ragging is when a piece of material is crumpled into an uneven ball and then pressed down over the wet glaze or paint. The finished effect is somewhat sharper than the first method. Different textures and effects can be achieved, depending on what type of material is used and how tightly it is rolled.

Dragging, one of the subtler finishes, which works very well on woodwork as well as walls, is a technique that has been popular for at least two hundred years. Like an informal wood-graining, a dragging effect is achieved by applying a dry brush, drawn downwards through wet paint or glaze to give a subtle, shadowy effect of very fine, irregular lines. Dragging does seem to look better when an oil-based glaze rather than a water-based one is used.

With all these paint techniques, it is sometimes better and more efficient for two people to work together, one brushing on the glaze or paint, the other brushing or dabbing. And, as with everything demanding manual skills, the more practice you have, the better the finished effect will be.

THIS PAGE In this Italian city apartment, paint effects have been used with subtle cleverness and a limited palette. In the kitchen, a warm yellow glaze has been applied over walls and cabinets with, at floor level, a band of warm terracotta. Glazed finishes can actually be very practical as they are usually sealed with clear varnish, which means that they can be easily cleaned. In a bedroom, the wall has been divided into panels of colour; a broad terracotta surround divides rich saffron-yellow walls, within which are panels lightly washed in a pale yellow-green. There is an interesting balance between the formal and informal here.

The important thing with all these finishes, particularly ragging, is to be subtle in both the choice of colour and the amount of pressure used when wielding the decorative tool. In the 1980s, when paint effects were first rediscovered, the most ghastly combinations sprung up, featuring surfaces covered with sharp and unconsidered stabs of contrasting colour, the whole looking as it suffered from an outbreak of a particularly infectious, virulent disease.

There are, of course, many other types of time-honoured painting techniques that have been perfected over the centuries. It is possible – and generally easier than two hundred years ago – to use colour to represent any surface in the natural world. It might be a wood-grained effect – anything from maple to burr walnut – or it might be mottled tortoiseshell, leather, malachite or lapis lazuli, a million types of marble, or even varying degrees of rust and age. Skill is needed, of course, and, at this level, an artistic bent also – but all is possible.

Equally possible is using colour in paint form to add surface decoration and pattern to a room. Both freehand and guided pattern can be applied to create a design or a trompe l'oeil effect that will enhance or correct the proportions of the room, or merely give pleasure. Freehand painting is difficult – but not quite as difficult as it might seem, particularly if you are relaxed about the direction it will follow. One of the simplest devices is to add fine coloured lines to correct architectural proportions and decorative faults. Where a skirting board is the wrong depth, particularly when it is too shallow, it can be corrected with one or even two bands of colour painted above it – either in the same colour as the board or as a contrast. Similarly, many rooms today are designed without dado rails, or have had them removed. Although many modern rooms do not need them, as the ceilings are lower than formerly, some rooms (particularly nineteenth-century ones) do. The dado rails in these houses balanced the proportions of the room and, once removed in the name of modernization, the room can become lopsided and out of proportion. The addition of bands of painted colour can give the impression of structure, particularly when the bands of

THIS PAGE In this golden living room designed by Geraldine Prieur, the walls have been prepared with a base coat of pale yellow, over which a glaze of cool orange has been applied. Around the room, stencilled in airy golden columns, are Prieur's interpretation of classical volutes and acanthus leaves, which, in appearance, are very close to her own favoured motif – the arabesque – which she uses on many of the ceramics, glass and other decorative accessories she designs.

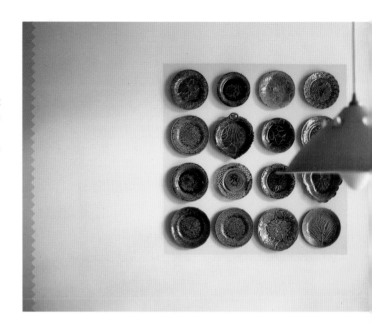

THIS PAGE Colour finishes do not have to be complicated. Here, blocks of colour are used to achieve the desired effect. The brilliantly simple device of hanging a collection of majolica plates against a coloured panel happened after the owner tried them against the yellow wall; unhappy with the combination, she applied, in that place only, a new colour, chosen to go with the plates. Her manner of hand-painting a zigzag border between changing paint colour is equally simple and equally pleasing.

colour are shadowed with a deeper tone, in a simple trompe l'oeil effect.

Simple, or even quite complex, panelling also can be painted onto walls to correct the proportions and add an instant sense of period. And, once emboldened by the success of these small forays into decorative painting, you might then go on to cover a wall, or indeed an entire hall, in hand-painted stripes. Stripes have been fashionable since the eighteenth century; unsurprisingly, since they immediately add distinction to any room. And anyone who appreciates stripes prefers them hand-painted – the slight unevenness, the variations in tone, the way the colour changes with the light, these all add up to an effect that is miles away from the bland uniformity of striped wallpaper.

Alternatively, if you prefer more pattern and colour, a stencil can be used to create repeated patterns in several colours over a large area. Stencils are not a new way to create pattern. In fact, they were probably used by the early Egyptians and the Romans. They were certainly used in medieval Britain and, famously, they were employed by early settlers in America on furniture, floors and walls. Stencils are usually sprayed or stippled onto the surface and can be used to make something as simple as a narrow border or something as complex as making a whole room appear to be lined with antique damask.

SUPPLIERS

Contemporary Paints

Brats
281 King's Road
London SW3 5EW
020 7351 7674 for mail order
www.brats.co.uk
Specialist paints, including the Mediterranean
Palette and the Chalk Collection

Casa Paint Company
01296 770139 for mail order
www.casa.co.uk
Traditional Mediterranean-style paints with a
matt, chalky finish. Also water-based acrylic,
fabric paint and a tile and melamine primer

Dacorum Colour Supplies
2–3 Mark Road
Hemel Hempstead
Hertfordshire HP2 7BN
01442 231261
Paints and accessories

Fired Earth
Twyford Mill
Oxford Road, Adderbury
Oxon OX17 3HP
01295 812088 for stockists
www.firedearth.co.uk
Historical and modern colours, including ranges
designed by Kevin McCloud and Kelly Hoppen
and the V&A's Historic Colours range

Foxell & James
57 Farringdon Road
London EC1M 3JB
020 7405 0152
Paints, scumbles and glazes

Grand Illusions
41 Crown Road
St Margarets
Middlesex TW1 3EE
01747 854092 for mail order

HABITAT
196 Tottenham Court Road
London W1T 9LD
020 7631 3880
0845 601 0740 for branches
www.habitat.net

Johnstone's Paints
Huddersfield Road
Birstall, Batley
W. Yorks WF17 9XA
01924 354600 for stockists
Over 1000 shades to choose from, plus a
free matching service

Macpherson Paints
Unit 2–3
Brough Parkway
Newcastle NE6 2YF
0191 265 7321

Ray Munn
13–15 Davies Street
London W1Y 1LN
020 7493 9333
861–863 Fulham Road
London SW6 5HP
020 7736 9876
www.raymunn.co.uk
Quality paints and accessories. Call for brochure

John Oliver Ltd
33 Pembridge Road
London W11 3HG
020 7221 6466
www.johnoliver.co.uk
Paints and original wallpaper designs in seriously
historical and wildly contemporary colours

The Paint Library
5 Elystan Street
London SW3 3NT
020 7823 7755 for mail order
www.paintlibrary.co.uk
Wide range, from muted shades to metallics; plus
Architectural Colours and Nina Campbell paints

Paint Magic
01273 747980 for branches

Paint Service Company
19 Eccleston Street
London SW1W 9LX
020 7730 6408
Glazes, stains and specialist brushes

Papers & Paints
4 Park Walk
London SW10 0AD
020 7352 8626
Excellent choice, including Historical Colour
range and computerized colour-matching service

Relics of Witney
35 Bridge Street
Witney OX8 6DA
01993 704611 for mail order
www.tryrelics.co.uk
Traditional and modern ranges, plus materials
for specialist paint effects

Historic Paints

Lawrence T Bridgeman
01924 413813 for stockists and mail order
Shaker- and American Colonial-style milk paints

British Museum Shop
020 7637 9449
www.britishmuseum.co.uk
30 colours inspired by ancient Egyptian, Greek,
Roman, Celtic and Far Eastern cultures, including
a rich Tibetan gold and a deep cobalt blue

Jane Churchill Interiors
81 Pimlico Road
London SW1W 8PH
020 7730 8564 for showroom
020 8877 6400 for stockists

Cole & Son
142–144 Offord Road
London N1 1NS
020 7607 4288
Paints, lime washes and wallpapers

Craig & Rose
Unit 17, Stuartfield Industrial Estate
New Haven Road
Edinburgh EH6 5RQ
0131 530 4045 for shop
01383 740011 for mail order
Decorative and industrial paints, historical and
metallic ranges, plus swimming-pool paints

Farrow & Ball
Uddens Estate
Wimborne
Dorset BH21 7NL
01202 876141
www.farrow-ball.com
Traditional papers and paints; manufacturer of
National Trust, Laura Ashley, Jane Churchill and
Designers Guild ranges

Francesca's Lime Wash
Unit 24a, Battersea Business Centre
99–109 Lavender Hill
London SW11 5QL
020 7228 7594 for mail order
www.francescaspaint.com
Open by appointment. Traditional lime wash and
milk paint

Potmolen Paints
27 Woodcock Industrial Estate
Warminster
Wilts BA12 9DX
01985 213960 for mail order
Distemper, lime wash, size, lime putty and whiting

The Old Village Paint Store
01543 480669 for mail order
Shaker-inspired and Heritage Village Colours
collections imported from America

Rose of Jericho
01935 83676 for mail order
www.rose-of-jericho.demon.co.uk
Muted paints, lime wash and distemper made
to traditional recipes

Shaker Ltd
72–3 Marylebone High Street
London W1M 3AR
020 7935 9461
www.shaker.co.uk
Paints in American Shaker colours

Annie Sloan's Traditional Paint Range
117 London Road
Headington
Oxford OX3 9HZ
01865 768666 for showroom
0870 6010082 for stockists and mail order
www.anniesloan.com
Modern and traditional decorative and wall
paints. Courses for amateur and professional
interior decorators

Zoffany
Chelsea Harbour Design Centre
Lots Road
London SW10 0XE
020 7349 0043 for showroom
01923 710680 for stockists
www.zoffany.co.uk

Eco-Friendly Paints

Auro Organic Paint Supplies Ltd
Unit 2, Pamphillions Farm
Purton End
Debden
Saffron Walden
Essex CB11 3JT
01799 543077
www.auroorganic.co.uk
Natural and eco-friendly paints

Natural Building Technologies
Cholsey Grange
Ibstone, High Wycombe
Bucks HP14 3XT
01491 638911
www.natural-building.co.uk
Paints, varnishes, oils and waxes, including
casein wall paint, historic-based glosses and
ecological emulsions

Nutshell Natural Paints
01364 73801 for mail order
www.naturalpaints.com
Ecologically sound paints, including a casein
milk paint and a durable eco-emulsion

Other Specialist Paint Products

Beckers
020 7736 98760
Masonry paint and exterior glosses which can be
mixed to any colour. Also wood stains

C. Brewer & Sons Ltd
327 Putney Bridge Road
London SW15 2PG
020 8788 9335
A comprehensive range, including scumbles,
glazes and metallic paints

Brodie & Middleton
68 Drury Lane
London WC2B 5SP
020 7836 3289
Pigments and specialist supplies

L. Cornelissen & Son
105 Great Russell Street
London WC1B 3RY
020 7636 1045
Artist's acrylics, powder pigments, gilding
materials and brushes

Hammerite Products
01661 830000
www.hammerite.com
Paint for metal

Holman Specialist Paints
01793 511537
Vast range, including vibrant colours for masonry and wood, such as fuchsia pink and cobalt blue. Also wood stains and industrial coatings

Oikos
020 8358 6220
Decorsil range of masonry paint in 320 colours which can also be mixed to the colour of your choice. Enamels and metallics for metal and woodwork

Pavillion Originals
6a Howe Street
Edinburgh EH3 6TD
0131 225 3590
Paints, glazes, stencils and specialist products

E. Ploton Ltd
273 Archway Road
London N6 5AA
020 8348 2838
Artists acrylics and gilding materials

Sandtex
01254 704 951
Masonry paint in smooth or textured finishes, plus one-coat or gloss finishes; 60 colour specialist paints for terracotta, stone and brickwork

Simoniz International
01637 871171 for stockists
Car paints

Tor Coatings
0191 410 6611 for stockists
www.tor-coatings.com
Manufacturer of specialist paints, including masonry, enamel and Ardenbrite gold, silver and other metallic paints

Courses on Paint Techniques

Friend or Faux
28 Earsham Street
Bungay
Suffolk NR35 1AG
01986 896170
Individual classes on paint effects

KLC School of Interior Design
Unit 503, 5th floor (North entrance)
The Chambers, Chelsea Harbour
London SW10 0XF
020 7602 8592
Courses on decorative paint finishes

Angela Shaw
Flexfor House
Hogs Back
Guildford
Surrey GU3 2JP
01483 810223
Courses in stencilling, paint finishes and gilding

Wallcoverings, Fabrics and Accessories

Alice & Astrid
71 Saltram Crescent
London W9 3JS
020 8960 7790
Textiles and bed-linen

Laura Ashley
256–258 Regent Street
London W1R 5DA
0870 5622 116 for branches
0800 868 100 for mail order
www.lauraashley.com

Bennison Fabrics
16 Holbein Place
London SW1W 8NL
020 7730 8076
New 'faded' linens with document prints

Bentley & Spens
1–2 Mornington Street
London NW1 7QD
020 7387 7374
Sparky modern fabrics, along with making-up service and design advice

Bernard Thorp
53 Chelsea Manor Street
London SW3 5RZ
020 7352 5457
Designs printed to your colours

Bryony Thomasson
19 Ackmar Road
London SW6 4UP
020 7731 3693
Handwoven sheets, covers and blankets for dyeing and furnishing

Nina Campbell
9 Walton Street
London SW3 2JD
020 7225 1011
www.ninacampbell.com
Beautifully designed, top-quality fabrics

Chalfont
222 Baker Street
London NW1 5RT
020 7935 7316
Professional dyers of curtains, bed-covers and loose covers

Chelsea Harbour Design Centre
108 The Chambers, Chelsea Harbour
London SW10 0XE
020 7351 4433
Lots and lots of fabric and trimmings trade showrooms

Colefax & Fowler
39 Brook Street
London W1Y 2JE
020 7493 2231 for stockists
Still the best at the English look, using many document prints, often re-coloured

The Conran Shop
81 Fulham Road
London SW3 6RD
020 7589 7401 for branches
www.conran.co.uk
Fabrics, furnishings and accessories

Thomas Dare
341 King's Road
London SW3 5ES
020 8542 1160 for stockists
Prints, weaves and trimmings

Decorative Fabrics Gallery
322 King's Road
London SW3 5UH
020 7823 3455
www.decorativefabrics.co.uk
www.monkwell.com
www.gpjbaker.co.uk
Monkwell and G P & J Baker showrooms, alongside a good range of quality accessories

Designers Guild
267 & 277 King's Road
London SW3 5EN
020 7351 5775
0845 602 1189 for mail order
www.designersguild.com

Anna French
343 King's Road
London SW3 5ES
020 7351 1126 for shop
020 7737 6555 for stockists
www.annafrench.co.uk
Fabrics, wallpapers, furniture and accessories

Pierre Frey
251–253 Fulham Road
London SW3 6HY
020 7376 5599
French prints and toile de Jouy

Heal's
196 Tottenham Court Road
London W1T 9LD
020 7636 1666 for branches
www.heals.co.uk
Modern fabrics, furnishings and accessories

The Isle Mill
Tower House, Ruthvenfield Road
Inveralmond, Perth PH1 3UN
01738 609090
Specialists in luxury neutrals and textured fabrics

Let it Loose
1 Milverton Street
London SE11 4AP
020 7582 1437
Loose covers made up, upholstery

Lelievre
1/19 Chelsea Harbour Design Centre
Chelsea Harbour
London SW10 0XE
020 7352 4798
Velvets, silks, damask, fur effects, prints

Lewis & Wood
5 The Green
Uley, Nr Dursley
Glos GL11 5SN
01453 860080
Heavyweight plain linens for curtains and upholstery

Liberty
214–220 Regent Street
London W1R 6AH
020 7734 1234
www.liberty-of-london.com
An eclectic mix of products for the home, including a wide range of fabrics and trimmings

Manuel Canovas
2 North Terrace
London SW3 2BA
020 7225 2298
Elegantly coloured fabrics by master designer

Natural Fabric Co.
127 High Street
Hungerford
Berks RG17 0DI
01488 684002
Fine range, from toile to tartan

Osborne & Little
304 King's Road
London SW3 5UH
020 7352 1456
Prints, wovens, sheers, silks and trimmings

Purves & Purves
220–224 Tottenham Court Road
London W1T 7QE
020 7580 8223 for mail order
www.purves.co.uk
Design-led furnishings and accessories

Pongees
28–30 Hoxton Square
London N1 6NN
020 7739 9130
Huge variety of silks, satins and georgettes, plus dyeing

George Spencer
29 Chapel Street
London SW1X 7DD
020 7235 1501
Natural, neutrals and textured fabrics; traditional woven fabrics, printed cottons and linens

The Suffolk Design House
Cotton Tree House
Yoxford Road
Westleton
Suffolk IP17 3AF
Curtains, loose covers and upholstery made up

Joanna Wood
48a Pimlico Road
London SW1W 8LP
020 7730 5064
www.joannawood.com

CREDITS

Architects and designers whose work is featured in this book:

Key: t = tel; f = fax; e = email; a = above; b = below; l = left; r = right; c = centre; ph = photographer

Nicholas Arbuthnott
Arbuthnott Ladenbury Architects
Architects & Urban Designers
15 Gosditch Street
Cirencester GL7 2AG
Pages: 1, 6, 24, 75, 150–151, 152–153, 153

Vanessa Arbuthnott Fabrics
The Tallet, Calmsden
Cirencester GL7 5ET
www.vanessaarbuthnott.co.uk
Pages: 1, 6, 24, 75, 150–151, 152–153, 153

John Barman Inc.
Interior Design
500 Park Avenue
New York, NY 10022, USA
t. +1 212 838 9443 / f. +1 212 838 4028
e. john@barman.com
www.johnbarman.com
Pages: 140–143

Roberto Bergero
Interior Designer
4 rue St. Gilles
75003 Paris, France
t. +33 1 42 72 03 51
e. robertobergero@club-internet.fr
Pages: 3 inset cl & inset r, 26 b, 36–37, 37, 55, 117

Bruce Bierman Design, Inc.
Residential Interior Design firm
29 West 15th Street
New York, NY 10011, USA
t. +1 212 243 1935 / f. +1 212 243 6615
www.Biermandesign.com
Pages: 52 c, 56–57

Hugh Broughton Architects
Award-winning architects
4 Addison Bridge Place
London W14 8XP
t. 020 7602 8840
f. 020 7602 5254
e. hugh@hbarchitects.demon.co.uk
Pages: 62–63

Buildboro
Design & Build
Unit 4, Iliffe Yard
Crampton Street
London, SE17 3QA
t. 020 7708 2538 / f. 020 7277 2104
e. gordanamandic@buildboro.co.uk
e. petertyler@buildboro.co.uk
www.buildboro.co.uk
Pages: 52 b, 70–71, 154–155, 180 al

Cabot Design Ltd.
Interior Design
1925 Seventh Avenue, Suite 7I
New York, NY 10026, USA
t. +1 212 222 9488
e. eocabot@aol.com
Pages: 7 bl, 26 a, 38 b, 39, 58–59, 59, 76, 77 a, 88 a, 94–95, 102 c, 109, 114, 114–115

Piero Castellini Baldissera
Studio Castellini
Via Morozzo della Rocca, 5
20123 Milan, Italy
Pages: 73

Circus Architects
Unit 1, Summer Street
London EC1R 5BD
t. 020 7833 1999
Pages: 110

Country House Walks Ltd.
Self-catering accommodation/weekend breaks
The Tallet, Calmsden
Cirencester GL7 5ET
www.thetallet.co.uk
Pages: 1, 6, 24, 75, 150–151, 152–153, 153

Cowper Griffith Associates
Chartered Architects
15 High Street
Whittlesford
Cambridge CB2 4LT
Pages: 170–171

Gloss Ltd.
Designers of home accessories
274 Portobello Road
London W10 5TE
t. 020 8960 4146 / f. 020 8960 4842
e. pascale@glossltd.u-net.com
Pages: 54, 65, 101 bc, 172–173, 173

James Gorst Architects
35 Lambs Conduit Street
London WC1N 3NG
t. 020 7831 8300
Pages: 47

Yves Halard
Interior Decoration
27 Quai de la Tournelle
75005 Paris, France
t. +33 1 44 07 14 00 / f. +33 1 44 07 10 30
Pages: 3 inset l, 58, 68, 69 ar & b, 88 b, 90–91, 97, 179 a & br

HM2 Architects
Architects & Designers
33–37 Charterhouse Square
London EC1M 6EA
t. 020 7600 5151 / f. 020 7600 1092
e. andrew.hanson@harper-mackay.co.uk
www.harper-mackay.co.uk
Pages: 160–163

Hut Sachs Studio
Architecture & Interior Design
414 Broadway

New York, NY 10013, USA
t. +1 212 219 1567 / f. +1 212 219 1677
e. hutsachs@hutsachs.com
www.hutsachs.com
Pages: 74 a, 81, 102 b, 119

Janie Jackson
Stylist/Designer
Parma Lilac
Children's nursery furnishings & accessories
t. 020 8960 9239
Pages: 39

Jacksons
5 All Saints Road
London W11 1HA
t. 020 7792 8336
Pages: 72 br

Eric Liftin
Mesh Architecture
Architecture & web-site design & development
555 Eighth Avenue, 14th floor
New York, NY 10013, USA
t. +1 212 965 1974 / f. +1 212 941 7478
e. info@mesh-arc.com
www.mesh-arc.com
Pages:.100

Moneo Brock Studio
Architecture & Interior Design
371 Broadway, 2nd Floor
New York, NY 10013, USA
t. +1 212 625 0308 / f. +1 212 625 0309
e. moneof@aol.com
Pages: 74 a, 81, 88 c, 101 a, 102 b, 119

Moss Co. Architects
Specialist conservator of early buildings, architectural, constructional and decorative finishes.
Brookgate, Pleasley
Shrewsbury SY5 0UY
Pages: 18 b

Mullman Seidman Architects
Architecture & Interior Design
443 Greenwich Street
New York, NY 10013, USA
t. +1 212 431 0770 / f. +1 212 431 8428
e. mullseid@monmouth.com
Pages: 40 c, 42–43, 169 al

Chris Ohrstrom
Historic Paints Ltd.
Burr Tavern
Route 1, PO Box 474
East Meredith
New York, NY 13757, USA
Pages: 19 c

Jennifer Post Design Inc.
Spatial & Interior Designer
25 East 67th Street, 8D
New York, NY 10021, USA
t. +1 212 734 7994 / f. +1 212 396 2450
e. jpostdesign@aol.com
Pages: 2–3, 26 c, 27, 28–29, 29–30, 32, 34, 49–51, 158, 179 bl

Géraldine Prieur
An interior designer fascinated with colour
7 rue Faraday
75017 Paris, France
t. +33 1 44 40 29 12 / f. +33 1 44 40 29 17
Pages: 53, 60–61, 103, 134–135, 182 a & br, 184

Lena Proudlock
Denim in Style, Drews House, Leighterton
Gloucestershire GL8 8UN
t./f. 01666 890230
Pages: 72 ar, 86–87

Sequana
64 avenue de la Motte Picquet
75015 Paris, France
t. +33 1 45 66 58 40 / f. +33 1 45 67 99 81
e. sequana@wanadoo.fr
Pages: 128–129

Stickland Coombe Architecture
Chartered architects who have completed over 40 projects for private clients in London
258 Lavender Hill
London SW11 1LJ
t. 020 7924 1699 / f. 0207652 1788
e. nick@scadesign.freeserve.co.uk
Pages: 4 b, 33, 35, 80, 84, 169 ar & b, 174–175

Touch Interior Design
t. 020 7498 6409
Pages: 7 br, 38 al & ar, 40 a, 48, 48–49, 130–133

Urban Research Laboratory
Architects
3 Plantain Place, Crosby Row
London SE1 1YN
t. 020 7403 2929
e. jeff@urbanresearchlab.com
Pages: 3 inset cr, 52 a, 64, 74 b, 85, 120–121, 136–139

Hervé Vermesch
Architect
50 rue Bichat
75010 Paris, France
t. +33 1 42 01 39 39
Pages: 113

Miv Watts at House Bait
Interior Decoration, lime-wash-painted furniture, country antiques from around the world
Market Place, Burnham Market
Norfolk, PE31 8HV
t. 01328 730557 / f. 01485 528970
e. miv.watts@virgin.net
Pages: 45, 77 b, 89, 181 a & bl

The Webb-Deane-Stevens Museum
211 Main Street
Wethersfield, CT 06109, USA
Pages: 19 a

Voon Wong Architects
Unit 27, 1 Stannary Street
London SE11 4AD
t. 020 7587 0116 / f. 020 7840 0178
e. voon@dircon.co.uk
Pages: 31 bl & br, 79, 156–157, 164–167

PICTURE CREDITS

1 The Arbuthnott family's house near Cirencester designed by Nicholas Arbuthnott, fabrics designed by Vanessa Arbuthnott; 2–3 Jennifer & Geoffrey Symonds' apartment in New York designed by Jennifer Post Design; 3 inset l Interior Designer and Managing Director of the Société Yves Halard, Michelle Halard's own apartment in Paris; 3 inset cl & r Interior Designer Roberto Bergero's own apartment in Paris; 3 inset c Donata Sartorio's apartment in Milan; 3 inset cr Richard Oyarzarbal's apartment in London designed by Urban Research Laboratory; 4 a Gail & Barry Stephens' house in London; 4 b Alannah Weston's house in London designed by Stickland Coombe Architecture; 5 Lindsay Taylor's apartment in Glasgow; 6 The Arbuthnott family's house near Cirencester designed by Nicholas Arbuthnott, fabrics designed by Vanessa Arbuthnott; 7 bl Warner Johnson's apartment in New York designed by Edward Cabot of Cabot Design Ltd.; 7 br Katie Bassford King's house in London designed by Touch Interior Design; 9 *Colour Globes for Copper, Aquatint and Watercolour* (w/c on paper) by Philipp Otto Runge (1777–1810) Hamburg Kunsthalle, Hamburg, Germany/Bridgeman Art Library; 11 Marilea & Guido Somarè's apartment in Milan; 12 The Art Archive/Musée d'Orsay/Dagli Orti; 13 a *Portrait of Cardinal Carlo de Medici* by Andrea Mantegna (1431–1506) Galleria degli Uffizi, Florence, Italy/Bridgeman Art Library; 13 b The Art Archive/Musée d'Orsay/Dagli Orti; 14 al, c & b ph. Jerry Harper; 14 ar ph. Pia Tryde; 15 a Edifice, London ; 15 b Peter Rayner/Axiom Photographic Agency; 16 a ph. James Merrell; 16 b Ancient Art & Architecture Collection Ltd.; 17 l The Art Archive/Musée Condé, Chantilly/Josse; 17 r Cephas/Hervé Champollion; 18 a *Baptism of Christ (& 2 details)* 1450s (tempera on panel) by Piero della Francesca (c. 1419/21–92) National Gallery, London, UK/Bridgeman Art Library; 18 b ph. James Merrell/Moss Co. Architects; 19 a ph. James Merrell/The Webb-Deane-Stevens Museum; 19 c ph. James Merrell/Chris Ohrstrom, Historic Paints Ltd.; 19 b The National Trust Photographic Library/Andreas von Einsiedel; 20 l ph. James Merrell/Lillian Williams' chateau in Normandy, France; 20 r Courtesy of the Trustees of the Sir John Soames Museum; 21 a 'Wandle' printed fabric manufactured by Morris and Co. and Aymer Vallance, from *The Art of William Morris*, pub. 1897 by William Morris (1834–96) Calmann & King, London, UK/Bridgeman Art Library; 21 b David Hockney, *Beverly Hills Housewife*, 1966, Acrylic on canvas, 72 x 144", (c) David Hockney; 22 Gail & Barry Stephens' house in London; 24 The Arbuthnott family's house near Cirencester designed by Nicholas Arbuthnott, fabrics designed by Vanessa Arbuthnott; 26 a Warner Johnson's apartment in New York designed by Edward Cabot of Cabot Design Ltd.; 26 c Jennifer & Geoffrey Symonds' apartment in New York designed by Jennifer Post Design; 26 b Interior Designer Roberto Bergero's own apartment in Paris; 27 Stanley & Nancy Grossman's apartment in New York designed by Jennifer Post Design; 28–29 & 29–30 Jennifer & Geoffrey Symonds' apartment in New York designed by Jennifer Post Design; 31 bl & br The architect Voon Wong's own apartment in London; 32 Jennifer & Geoffrey Symonds' apartment in New York designed by Jennifer Post Design; 33 Alannah Weston's house in London designed by Stickland Coombe Architecture; 34 Stanley & Nancy Grossman's apartment in New York designed by Jennifer Post Design; 35 Alannah Weston's house in London designed by Stickland Coombe Architecture; 36 a & b Toia Saibene's apartment in Milan; 36–37 & 37 Interior Designer Roberto Bergero's own apartment in Paris; 38 al & ar Katie Bassford King's house in London designed by Touch Interior Design; 38 b & 39 Warner Johnson's apartment in New York designed by Edward Cabot of Cabot Design Ltd.; 40 a Katie Bassford King's house in London designed by Touch Interior Design; 40 c Margot Feldman's house in New York designed by Patricia Seidman of Mullman Seidman Architects; 40 b Gail & Barry Stephens' house in London; 41 ph. James Merrell/Janie Jackson, stylist/designer; 42–43 Margot Feldman's house in New York designed by Patricia Seidman of Mullman Seidman Architects; 44 Gail & Barry Stephens' house in London; 45 Miv Watts' house in Norfolk; 46 ph. James Merrell/Bill Blass, New York; 47 ph. Andrew Wood/An apartment in London designed by James Gorst; 48 & 48–49 Katie Bassford King's house in London designed by Touch Interior Design; 49–51 Stanley & Nancy Grossman's apartment in New York designed by Jennifer Post Design; 52 a Richard Oyarzarbal's apartment in London designed by Urban Research Laboratory; 52 c New York apartment designed by Bruce Bierman; 52 b Selworthy apartment in London designed by Gordana Mandic & Peter Tyler at Buildboro (www.buildboro.co.uk); 53 Géraldine Prieur's apartment in Paris, an Interior Designer fascinated with colour; 54 Owner of Gloss, Pascale Bredillet's own apartment in London; 55 Interior Designer Roberto Bergero's own apartment in Paris; 56–57 New York apartment designed by Bruce Bierman; 58 Interior Designer and Managing Director of the Société Yves Halard, Michelle Halard's own apartment in Paris; 58–59 & 59 Warner Johnson's apartment in New York designed by Edward Cabot of Cabot Design Ltd.; 60–61 Géraldine Prieur's apartment in Paris, an Interior Designer fascinated with colour; 62–63 Private apartment in London designed by Hugh Broughton Architects; 64 Richard Oyarzarbal's apartment in London designed by Urban Research Laboratory; 65 Owner of Gloss, Pascale Bredillet's own apartment in London; 66–67 Lisa Fine's apartment in Paris; 68 & 69 ar & b Interior Designer and Managing Director of the Société Yves Halard, Michelle Halard's own apartment in Paris; 70–71 Selworthy apartment in London designed by Gordana Mandic & Peter Tyler at Buildboro (www.buildboro.co.uk); 72 al ph. Henry Bourne; 72 ar ph. Polly Wreford/Lena Proudlock's house in Gloucestershire; 72 br ph. Polly Wreford/Louise Jackson's house in London; 73 ph. Fritz von der Schulenburg/Piero Castellini Baldissera's house in Montalcino, Siena; 74 a Maria Jesus Polanco's apartment in New York designed by Hut Sachs Studio in collaboration with Moneo Brock Studio; 74 c Toia Saibene's apartment in Milan; 74 b Richard Oyarzarbal's apartment in London designed by Urban Research Laboratory; 75 The Arbuthnott family's house near Cirencester designed by Nicholas Arbuthnott, fabrics designed by Vanessa Arbuthnott; 76 & 77 a Warner Johnson's apartment in New York designed by Edward Cabot of Cabot Design Ltd.; 77 b Miv Watts' house in Norfolk; 78 Andrew Wallace's house in London; 79 The architect Voon Wong's own apartment in London; 80 Alannah Weston's house in London designed by Stickland Coombe Architecture; 81 Maria Jesus Polanco's apartment in New York designed by Hut Sachs Studio in collaboration with Moneo Brock Studio; 82 a & 83 Marilea & Guido Somarè's apartment in Milan; 82 bl, bc & br Toia Saibene's apartment in Milan; 84 Alannah Weston's house in London designed by Stickland Coombe Architecture; 85 Richard Oyarzarbal's apartment in London designed by Urban Research Laboratory; 86–87 ph. Simon Upton/Lena Proudlock's house in Gloucestershire; 88 a Warner Johnson's apartment in New York designed by Edward Cabot of Cabot Design Ltd.; 88 c Hudson Street Loft in New York designed by Moneo Brock Studio; 88 b Interior Designer and Managing Director of the Société Yves Halard, Michelle Halard's own apartment in Paris; 89 Miv Watts' house in Norfolk; 90–91 Interior Designer and Managing Director of the Société Yves Halard, Michelle Halard's own apartment in Paris; 92–93 ph. James Merrell; 94–95 Warner Johnson's apartment in New York designed by Edward Cabot of Cabot Design Ltd.; 96 a Gail & Barry Stephens' house in London; 96 bl & br ph. Pia Tryde; 97 Interior Designer and Managing Director of the Société Yves Halard, Michelle Halard's own apartment in Paris; 98–99 Donata Sartorio's apartment in Milan; 100 Architect Eric Liftin's own apartment in New York; 101 a Hudson Street Loft in New York designed by Moneo Brock Studio; 101 bc Owner of Gloss, Pascale Bredillet's own apartment in London; 101 br ph. Pia Tryde; 102 a Donata Sartorio's apartment in Milan; 102 c Warner Johnson's apartment in New York designed by Edward Cabot of Cabot Design Ltd.; 102 b Maria Jesus Polanco's apartment in New York designed by Hut Sachs Studio in collaboration with Moneo Brock Studio; 103 An apartment in Paris designed by Géraldine Prieur, an Interior Designer fascinated with colour; 104–105 Donata Sartorio's apartment in Milan; 106–107 ph. James Merrell/Sally Butler's house in London; 108 Toia Saibene's apartment in Milan; 109 Warner Johnson's apartment in New York designed by Edward Cabot of Cabot Design Ltd.; 110 ph. Ray Main/John Howell's loft in London designed by Circus Architects; 110–111 ph. Chris Everard/An apartment in London designed by Littman Goddard Hogarth, light courtesy of Skandium; 111 a ph. Andrew Wood/An apartment in London designed by Littman Goddard Hogarth; 111 b ph. Chris Everard/An apartment in London designed by Littman Goddard Hogarth, light courtesy of SCP; 112 ph. James Merrell/Vicky & Simon Young's house in Northumberland; 113 ph. James Merrell/An apartment in Paris designed by Hervé Vermesch; 114 & 114–115 Warner Johnson's apartment in New York designed by Edward Cabot of Cabot Design Ltd.; 115 ph. Andrew Wood/Kurt Bredenbeck's apartment at the Barbican, London; 116 Lisa Fine's apartment in Paris; 117 Interior Designer Roberto Bergero's own apartment in Paris; 118 Lisa Fine's apartment in Paris; 119 Maria Jesus Polanco's apartment in New York designed by Hut Sachs Studio in collaboration with Moneo Brock Studio; 120–121 Richard Oyarzarbal's apartment in London designed by Urban Research Laboratory; 122 Andrew Wallace's house in London; 124–127 Lindsay Taylor's apartment in Glasgow; 128 al & ar & 129 ph. Andrew Wood/Mary Shaw's Sequana apartment in Paris; 128 b The Irish Picture Library; 130–133 Katie Bassford King's house in London designed by Touch Interior Design; 134–135 Géraldine Prieur's apartment in Paris, an Interior Designer fascinated with colour; 136–139 Richard Oyarzarbal's apartment in London designed by Urban Research Laboratory; 140–143 Interior Designer John Barman's own apartment in New York; 144–147 Director of design consultants Graven Images, Janice Kirkpatrick's apartment in Glasgow; 148–149 Andrew Wallace's house in London; 150–151 The Arbuthnott family's house near Cirencester designed by Nicholas Arbuthnott, fabrics designed by Vanessa Arbuthnott; 152 ph. James Merrell; 152–153 & 153 The Arbuthnott family's house near Cirencester designed by Nicholas Arbuthnott, fabrics designed by Vanessa Arbuthnott; 154–155 Selworthy apartment in London designed by Gordana Mandic & Peter Tyler at Buildboro (www.buildboro.co.uk); 156–157 The architect Voon Wong's own apartment in London; 158 Stanley & Nancy Grossman's apartment in New York designed by Jennifer Post Design; 160–163 ph. Christopher Drake/Juan Corbella'a apartment in London designed by HM2, Richard Webb with Andrew Hanson; 164–167 The architect Voon Wong's own apartment in London; 168 Andrew Wallace's house in London; 169 al Margot Feldman's house in New York designed by Patricia Seidman of Mullman Seidman Architects; 169 ar & b Alannah Weston's house in London designed by Stickland Coombe Architecture; 170–171 ph. Simon Upton/A house in Norfolk designed by Chris Cowper of Cowper Griffith Associates; 172 b Gail & Barry Stephens' house in London; 172–173 & 173 Owner of Gloss, Pascale Bredillet's own apartment in London; 174–175 Alannah Weston's house in London designed by Stickland Coombe Architecture; 176–177 Director of design consultants Graven Images, Janice Kirkpatrick's apartment in Glasgow; 178 Marilea & Guido Somarè's apartment in Milan; 179 a & br Interior Designer and Managing Director of the Société Yves Halard, Michelle Halard's own apartment in Paris; 179 bl Stanley & Nancy Grossman's apartment in New York designed by Jennifer Post Design; 180 a Selworthy apartment in London designed by Gordana Mandic & Peter Tyler at Buildboro (www.buildboro.co.uk); 181 Miv Watts' house in Norfolk; 182 Géraldine Prieur's apartment in Paris, an Interior Designer fascinated with colour; 183 Donata Sartorio's apartment in Milan; 184 An apartment in Paris designed by Géraldine Prieur, an Interior Designer fascinated with colour; 185 Lindsay Taylor's apartment in Glasgow; 192 Interior Designer John Barman's own apartment in New York

All photography by Alan Williams unless otherwise stated.
In addition to those mentioned above, the publisher would like to thank: Enrica Stabile in Milan, Jon Geir and Inger Høyersten, and the Heddal-og Nottodden Museum in Norway.

INDEX

Figures in *italics* indicate captions.

Acknowledgements

Writing this book opened my eyes even further to the possibilities,

pleasures and sheer beauty of colour. I realised that one too often takes

colour for granted, both as it is found in the natural world, and as used in

decoration. Making this book look as good as it does was a team effort and

I would like, especially, to thank the ever-tranquil Sophie Bevan (at least

with me), Gabriella Le Grazie, Catherine Randy and Sarah Hepworth

for producing such a terrific book.